BUST-UP

BUST-UP

The uplifting tale of Otto Titzling and the development of the bra

Wallace Reyburn

Prentice-Hall, Inc.
Englewood Cliffs, N.J.

© Wallace Reyburn 1971

First published in 1971 by
Macdonald & Co. (Publishers) Ltd.
London W1

First American Edition published by
Prentice-Hall, Inc., 1972

Library of Congress Catalog Card Number : 72–179624

Printed and made in Great Britain by
A. Wheaton & Co., Exeter

ISBN : 0–13–108761–4

Contents

There are eight pages of photographs
between pages 58 and 59

*The author wishes to thank the following
for their help in providing illustrations for
this book:*

*Berlei (U.K.) Ltd, Gossards (Holdings) Ltd,
Silhouette (London) Ltd, The Corset Guild of Great Britain,
The Patent Office*

*Otto Titzling
as a young man*

1

The Young Titzling

Otto Titzling, inventor of the brassiere as we know it today, was born in Hamburg in 1884. He died in New York in 1942, an unhappy man. Men who had been contemporaries and, like him, pioneers in their own field, had lived to see their names become household words—men like George Stetson, Hugo Jantzen and Charlie Kotex. But not Titzling.

The word that became the accepted term for the revolutionary new form of women's undergarment was 'brassiere'. 'Titzling' had a certain vogue at the outset but soon fell into disrepute, undoubtedly a direct result of the long and bitterly contested court case which was a *cause célèbre* of the time, when Titzling sued the Frenchman, Philippe de Brassière, for infringement of patents.

Otto's father, Gustav Titzling, was a civil engineer who had migrated to America when Otto was three. The old man had specialised in bridge building and, being of an inventive turn of mind, had developed a type of easily erected sectional bridge with which he had much success. Early this century, with mechanised farming opening up in a big way, he had seen the need of farmers for such a thing to bridge the numerous creeks and ravines on their vast holdings. The safe, relatively cheap Titzling bridge became as well known to, say, an Idaho farmer as the Model T Ford. As his business thrived, the slogan 'Put your trust in a Titzling' was to be seen along the country roads from upper New York state to the Far West. And it was this slogan that was to cause friction between the old man and his son, when Otto started to make a name for himself in his own walk of life.

One evening a torrid row broke out between the two.

'It is bad enough,' said Gustav, 'that you went against my wishes in your choice of work. I had become resigned to that. But now, this is different. It is reflecting on me in the most embarrassing, disastrous way.'

'What do you mean?' asked Otto.

'I'll tell you what I mean : our agents out West report that people are making fun of our slogan, which has borne us in such good stead for 27 years now. On the hoardings they're changing "Put your trust in a Titzling" to "Put your bust in a Titzling".'

'That's rather good,' chuckled Otto.

'Rather good! I spend a whole lifetime trying to make the name Titzling mean something, and now . . .'

It was but one of the numerous scenes that were to take place between father and son, stemming from the earliest days of Otto's obvious disinterest in the family business.

The two elder sons, Stephan and Rudi, had without hesitation followed in father's footsteps. But not Otto. He had his eyes on other things. From an early age he would pore over the women's underwear section of the Sears-Roebuck catalogue, dreaming his dreams, formulating his ideas.

It was a great disappointment to Titzling senior when Otto came of age to work and decided he wanted to join his uncle, Louie Framer, who was in the garment trade.

'Young Otto has broken my heart,' Gustav said to his wife. 'Always our family has been in engineering or other such manly pursuits. And now young Otto wants to go off and fool around with women's clothes. He doesn't behave like a son of mine.'

Otto's mother would say nothing at such outbursts, merely sitting gazing wistfully out of the window and thinking back to the days of the Franco-Prussian war, when many a handsome young officer was billeted on families living in the path of battle.

She had a soft spot for Otto. She always sprang to his defence when the old man seized every opportunity to raise the roof about his youngest son, such occasions as when he stormed into the house after suffering what he felt had been a terrible indignity at his club. Apparently he had overheard a member saying to a friend : 'I hear his young son Otto's now working in a bloomer factory. I understand he's pulling down forty a week.' The ribald laughter at this was still ringing in his ears when he got home and his wife did her best to point out to him that the boy must be allowed to make his own way in life, come what may.

On the occasion of yet another row between Otto and his father, Otto had dared to voice the opinion that although not following his father into bridge building, he was nevertheless in a similar sort of business.

'A similar sort of business!' his father bellowed. 'By no stretch of the imagination can the construction of a suspension bridge be likened to the making of a – the making of *ein Buzumgershaft*!' [The old German word for a brassiere.]

'I don't agree,' said Otto. 'I have the same sort of problems that you have. Stress . . . load capacity . . . all those factors which have to be taken into consideration –'

'Get out!' his father had screamed.

This blast from Titzling senior, at an attempt by Mrs Titzling at a reconciliation between the two, was an echo of what had happened those years before when he had literally meant what he said. He did not want the young Otto around, unless he decided to come to his senses and join his brothers in the family business. Despite the pleadings of his wife, he had been adamant.

'You say the boy should be allowed to make his own way in life,' he said to her. 'Very well, let him do just that. He won't get anything from me from now on.'

'But you can't do that. He's your son.'

'I'm doing it. And bear this in mind. If I find you trying to slip him money, there'll be trouble. Do you understand?'

His wife could only shake her head sadly.

'And another thing. That sister of yours, married to that unbearable Framer specimen. You're not going to get her to look after him and give him money and –'

'She has enough to do with all her family to look after.'

'Well, just tell her, anyway. He's on his own. Do you understand? On his own.'

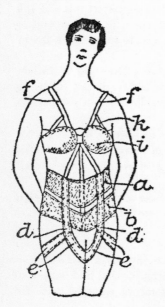

Support for Otto's claim that he was in the same sort of business as his father: a diagram of the points of stress in an early bra and girdle

'You're so cruel.'

'It's for his own good. He'll come to his senses soon enough when he sees that life isn't so simple as he thinks. When he can't make a go of things. You'll see."

'I doubt it, Gustav,' his wife said quietly. 'He's as stubborn as you are.'

And indeed Otto had not gone running back. From the time he had moved into the rooming house of Mrs Riley in New York that summer of 1910 he had been determined that he would not be dominated by his father and be forced to spend his life at work in which he was not the least bit interested. He would do what *he* wanted to do.

He was a serious-minded young man, inclined to be rather earnest. He was conscientious and ambitious. He did, however, have a relieving sense of humour and he was companionable. He made friends at the factory and in the trade in general and among those who stayed at his rooming house or came and went there. Not the least of his friends was a girl who lived in the room below his – a young lady who was to play an important part in his evolving of his brainchild.

Swanhilda in 1910

2

Swanhilda

Swanhilda Olafsen, who was of Icelandic descent, had come from
Minneapolis to New York to further her career as a singer. She was
a big girl. Not fat. Just big. She had a good figure but it was built
to a somewhat larger scale than that of girls whose antecedents were
not from those Northern climes. She was statuesque, Wagnerian.
Undoubtedly Wagnerian was the most appropriate way of putting
it, since opera was her great ambition and by this time she had
managed to make more than one appearance at the Met. 'Nothing
very grand yet,' she confessed. 'I haven't got beyond being just one
of the Rhine Maidens so far, but my time will come.'

Her chosen calling was not without effect on her figure. From her
earliest youth, when she first started taking singing lessons, she had
had the correct method of voice production dinned into her : 'From

6

the diaphragm! From the diaphragm!' Any singing teacher will tell you that men have a natural physical advantage over women in regard to this essential of having the voice well up from the base of the chest. Women have to work hard on it and the constant drawing in and expanding of the diaphragm cannot help but strengthen the muscles that support the bust and build it up. In the case of Swanhilda, already well endowed in that respect, it resulted in a bust that was spectacular in size. And, as we shall see, this was to form the jumping-off point for Otto Titzling's excursion into the evolving of an entirely new type of undergarment.

Otto found Swanhilda great fun. She was a cheerful sort of person and was good company. They saw a lot of each other, going out to eat together, to shows and walks in Central Park, and they would

Otto's breakthrough: a sketch for the prototype 'chest halter'

have long chats in the evening about their mutual interests. One of the places where they ate was a spot a couple of blocks away called the Gay Viking, where the food wasn't all that good but it did have the merit of being cheap. It was Mrs Riley's husband, an unemployed museum attendant, who coined the nickname by which she was known around the house when one evening he said to Otto, 'Haven't seen much of her these last couple of days; how's the Gay Viking?' But among her friends in operatic circles she was known affectionately if not too accurately as Swan. It was these friends of hers that he met when she got him to start taking an interest in music. Classical music, that is – opera, symphony and the other forms rather above the level of what was about the only type of music to be heard in the Titzling home, the Sousa marches that his father doted on because they were a real man's type of music and they carried his mind back to the military might of the Prussian army. Otto was always to be grateful to Swan for the widening of his musical vision by taking him to concerts and explaining things to him at the harmonium and with the victrola she had in her room.

He was even more grateful to her, of course, for triggering off his interest in inventing the bra, which was to come about in the following way.

The womenfolk at Mrs Riley's welcomed the fact that he was in women's underclothing since it meant that he could get drawers and corsets and so on for them and their friends at wholesale rates. The ordering was invariably done through Mrs Riley, partly because it meant that instead of bringing stuff home from the factory in dribs and drabs he could bring it in bulk lots and also, more important, one should bear in mind that this was the 1910s, when the tenets of propriety were such that no respectable young lady would ever dream of discussing such things as undies with a man : they fell into the category of articles which came to the purchaser "under plain cover". However, Mrs Riley being an older woman, it was all right.

One evening when Otto had brought home a new batch and she was checking through them against the list the girls had provided, she paused when she came to the pair of 'Sitwell' Side-Spring High-

Rise corsets, a new Framer product just on the market.

'This sort of thing really isn't of much help to Swanhilda,' she said.

'Why not?' asked Otto.

'Her you-know-whats. This is all right for the average girl. But it's up here –' Mrs Riley indicated her own poor offering, '– this is where Swanhilda, poor soul, needs real support.'

Otto took the Sitwell. 'But you see up here at the top, where it's moulded –'

'Quite inadequate for the Gay Viking. You know something, your people should make something specially for girls like her.'

It was just a passing comment. They went on to discuss other things. Mrs Riley, giving the top of a pair of pantaloons a good stretch, said that she hoped that the elastic would stand up better to washing than the last lot, because not only was it terribly embarrassing when without warning they suddenly drop to your ankles but also if it happened when you were running for a streetcar you could take a nasty tumble.

The list finally checked, Otto took his departure but that casual remark about Swanhilda stuck in his mind. If a girl like her had a special need in that respect, indeed why not do something about it?

A couple of days later he came back to Mrs Riley on the subject and she was able to give him some background, if not from direct knowledge at least from what she had heard and observed from the personal disclosures to which women are more prone than men.

'Since you're interested,' she said, 'I can tell you that it's no fun lugging those things around day in, day out.'

'I didn't realise.'

'Of course not. You men wouldn't. After a heavy day they can get painful.'

'They can?'

'Sure. They've got to have proper support. This fashion for slim waists is all very well. The corset manufacturers cater for that all right but they never seem to have given any thought for the woman who's really big up on top. And it's not only support. They'd like to look more shapely. That great big bolster you get when everything's bunched up by the top of the corset !'

The outcome of this was that he asked Mrs Riley to get some measurements from Swanhilda and he started working out in his mind just what could be done.

He would lie in bed thinking about Swanhilda's breasts. They kept him from sleep. How to evolve an effective chest halter that would at one and the same time give them much needed support and impart a shapeliness to the exterior contour, while still giving adequate freedom of movement. Designing the bloomers which Mrs Amelia Bloomer had brought into such favour was not really designing at all, since by then they had become very much stylised. Two to three yards of *crêpe de chine* depending on size and a couple of yards of knicker elastic, and you were in business. There were seasonal changes, of course, such as heavier material for winter wear, and the addition of a bit of lace here and an ornamental bow there according to how fanciful you wanted to be, but that was all there was to it. Now, however, he was starting from scratch. Designing a bust halter for Swanhilda was a real challenge.

Even today brassiere designers find it essential to do their work on the human form. Granted they can work out on the drawing board the initial concept of their new item but nobody has yet come up with a dummy that will say, 'Ouch, that's too tight under the arms' and such like. They must work with a live model. So it was that Otto, with bits and pieces of material he had borrowed from the factory, was able to do a mock-up of what he had in mind for Swan, but the only true test of whether it would work was to do a live run-through to see what modifications and improvements were needed.

It was a delicate matter and one which in the broaching of the subject his innate bashfulness made him hesitant. At the factory, when they gave a show for out-of-town buyers, the girls wandered around in the bloomers without anyone giving a thought to it. With Swanhilda it was different. They lived in the same rooming house, went out together for concerts and meals, had a nice friendly relationship that was in all ways quite proper, conforming to the rules of rectitude of those days long before the free-and-easy, permissive attitude of today, in that period when the moral tone was so high that it went to the extent of legs being referred to as 'nether extremities' and the bosom as 'the upper part of the body'. It was not easy to ask a nice girl like Swanhilda to lay aside the top portion of her clothing so that he could do a proper job on perfecting his brainchild.

One thing that did make it a bit simpler, however, was the fact that she would only be required to remove her blouse. As will be explained later in this book, intimate items such as corsets were not in those days worn next to the skin. They went on over the chemise or shift. So in evolving his new garment Otto had no reason to think of departing from this accepted procedure; it would go on over the top of the chemise. There would be no question of having to ask Swan to strip down to the buff.

At length courage was plucked up and one morning when she asked him what was the delay in letting her see what she knew he had planned for her, he told her that there was nothing much more he could do until he worked on it while fitting it on to her. She consented to this and that evening he found his way to her room with his cut-out pieces of material, tapes, pins, needle and thread.

No sooner was the blouse off than he could see at once where the trouble lay. Normally the high boned corset came right under the bosom, supporting it aided by the upper part of the chemise, which was so positioned when the corset was being put on that it was stretched tight enough to keep the bosom well up. But Swanhilda had overspill in the worst way. The conventional harnessing was quite ineffectual for her prodigious bust.

'Try this on,' said Otto. 'It's just tacked. We can take it apart and adjust it.'

She did not seem to know what precisely he had in mind for his oddly shaped garment, which had a complete band around the bottom rather than loose ends for fastening as today but apart from that was not a great deal different in essentials from the modern bra, if rather more cumbersome.

'You put it on over your head,' he explained, 'with one arm going through this loop and the other through this other loop.'

She got the idea and with a spirit of adventure hauled it down over her head and with a certain amount of swivelling of her shoulders and pulling back and forth here and there she managed to get things into position.

Otto drew his head back in appraisal. It did look a bit of a mess, what with bits of embroidery on the top of her camisole sticking out in various places and, being cut generously to her measurements on the basis that it was easier to take in than to let out, it tended to balloon out at the sides. But although it might be said to fit where it touched, he felt a little glow of excitement when he discounted these initial shortcomings in his mind's eye and realised that in essence it could do the job. Swan's bust was up and away, the pendulous effect eliminated, so that she was getting the required support, and the cut of the garment in two definite parts would, when he got it right, impart a separated shapeliness in pleasing contrast to

*The prototype 'chest halter' being wear-tested.
It was a success right from the start*

the previous amorphous bay-window effect. He was really on to something here!

'We'll have to take a tuck in here,' he said, cupping her left breast in his hand and smoothing the material down and across so that it gave a clean line.

'Oh, my God!'

'What did you say?'

'Nothing.'

With the other hand he smoothed the other side down. 'Now that's what we want,' he said.

'Oooooh!'

Intent on what he had been doing, trying to get it looking exactly as he had envisaged it, he now looked up at Swanhilda.

'What's the matter? It's not uncomfortable, is it?'

'No, no, no. It's not uncomfortable.'

Otto warmed to his work. With a mouthful of pins he took in tucks and gathers. He broke away the loose stitching where the shoulder-straps were attached in front and moved things up to pin the straps in new position. He tucked the loose bits of the camisole well down into the garment.

'What's wrong?' he asked, breaking off. 'You're shivering.'

'Am I?'

'You're shaking all over.'

'I don't know. I must have got a chill.'

'In mid-August?'

'A summer chill. Yes, that's probably what I've got. A summer chill."

'Well, we'd better stop and you can get dressed. If you feel chilly we shouldn't go on.'

'No, no, don't stop. You seem to be getting it right. I wouldn't want you to have to stop now.'

'But do you feel all right?'

'I'm fine now. See, it's passed. Probably just somebody walking over my grave.'

'Walking over your grave?'

'Yes. That's what they say, isn't it, when you suddenly get the shudders like that?'

'I guess so. Now, let's see.' He reviewed the situation and then suddenly checked himself. 'Say! I haven't asked you yet what *you* think about it. After all, it's for you.'

'I think it's wonderful.'

He reached out a hand. 'It looks a bit tight here.'

'No, that's all right.'

'What about across here?'

And in a moment, try as she might to keep her mind on the subject under discussion, it was too much for her. The shudders came back. More so now, culminating in her throwing all to the winds and bringing her arms around him and clutching him to her.

'Oh, Otto,' she said.

It was clear, after she had held him for a little while, rocking him gently to and fro, and then leaning back from him to look intently at him with a warm half-smile on her face, that something was expected of him. But he was hesitant.

He liked Swanhilda very much. She was a good friend to him in New York, where he needed friends. She was fun to go out with. She had introduced him to good music and the enjoyment to be derived from it. She had lent him money at times when he was short until next payday, as when he had gone overboard and bought that good looking knickerbocker suit. She was liberal with the ice-box cookies her mother sent her from Minneapolis. She was warm, generous, kindly. She was all those things. But he was just not attracted to her physically.

He did feel that the least he could do would be to give her a token kiss; it wouldn't hurt him. He would have thought twice about it if he had realised what the outcome would be. No sooner were his lips on hers than she seemed to have been hit by some of this new electric voltage which was fast taking over completely from gas power. A jolt went through her, she clasped him even more eagerly and her whole body became a hive of frenzied activity.

'Oh, Otto. Darling. I've waited and waited, longed and longed for this moment.'

Her lips were pressed on to his again, as forcibly as her arms encircled him. Then abruptly she released him and with frenzied movements started to pull his embryonic bra off up over her head. In the turmoil that was within her she had difficulty in becoming free of it, getting an elbow stuck and then getting the thing caught up in her hair before at length it was off. Otto made a mental note that he must do something about making it easier to get on and off.

Then, before he quite knew what was afoot, the top of her chemise was down, she was lying on the divan and there before him in their full splendour were the Swanhilda upperworks.

('Oh, dear. What am I letting myself in for? But she's such a nice kid and she's so good to me . . .')

Otto found himself enveloped in the prodigious bust. She stroked the back of his head and he could hear sounds of mellow contentment welling up from her. The tempo quickened.

('I really must call a halt.')

Raising himself from the doughy darkness, he looked up at her but before he had a chance to say anything the sight of his face seemed to induce a fresh upsurge in her. She took the hand he had tentatively placed on her skirt at the thigh and held it away as she made some rapid adjustments of her clothes and then replaced it. In impromptu love-making in those days this was a necessary feminine manoeuvre, since the multiplicity of underskirts, petticoats and so on made it like delving around trying to find something in an unmade bed.

'No, no,' said Otto, doing his best to make it sound like 'Let's not cheapen this moment' and feeling a complete heel at his duplicity.

However, it seemed to have the desired effect. The frenzy left her and she calmed down, no doubt on her reasoning that now that the first move had been made the glorious weeks ahead stretched invitingly before them and why rush things? She gave him a warm smile of understanding and kissed him tenderly.

In this mood he was able to say that he thought he should be getting back to his room and she held his hand affectionately as they went to the door.

'When shall we have my next fitting?' she asked.

Oh, dear. This would all crop up again. Why didn't he have the courage to tell her straight out that, sorry as he was to have to say it, there was just nothing there as far as he was concerned? And besides, at the moment one Martha Medina was fully occupying his mind in that field of endeavour. No, he just couldn't hurt Swan's feelings. She was so darn nice. He'd have to think of some way of breaking it to her gently. . . .

'I'll do some work on it at the factory,' he said, 'and I'll let you know.'

'All right, darling.'

She leaned forward to be kissed and, since it was safe enough now, he complied. He couldn't leave her unhappy.

'Good night, my sweet,' she said, content now to be left alone to the reflective enjoyment of something shared.

And Otto took his departure, feeling an utter cad.

For the next few days Otto was torn between his desire to get going on his project (he felt he was on to something : if it worked for Swanhilda why not for other women of her build . . . he could put it on the market with all sorts of promising possibilities) and the embarrassing situation he knew would be repeated at a further session with her.

What a pity it was that, fond of her as he was, she aroused no physical excitement in him. All would we well if she did. But the lack of chemistry between them as far as he was concerned was made even more pronounced in view of his interest in Martha Medina. This young lady he loved ardently. He was captivated, enthralled by her. She was the one he had his heart set on. Oddly enough, he reflected, it was he now who was like more than one girl he had fallen for who had rejected him because she felt nothing physical for him and/or her sights were set elsewhere. He knew how frustrated this could make a man feel, and now that he was doing the same thing to Swanhilda he felt deeply sorry for her. He would just have to work out some way in which he could soften the blow.

As things turned out, however, it was to be resolved at the very next fitting.

Things had started off unemotionally enough. She had greeted him with an embrace on his arrival in her room but he managed to offset that without much difficulty by at once getting her interested in his enthusiasm for the progress he had made on her new garment.

On the basis of meat course first, apple pie *à la mode* to follow, she went along with this and listened with interest as he explained that he had made a modification whereby there was not a complete band around the bottom, there were two loose ends at the back. Much more easily she could put it on by merely putting an arm through each loop and then with her hands up around the back secure it with a bow.

In practice, though, this didn't appear to be such a good idea. She was quick to point out something which would not necessarily occur to a man. No matter how neatly the bow was tied at the back, there would be a bump there plus the stray bits at the end which could not help but protrude on the back of her dress or blouse and spoil the line. Also it wasn't the easiest thing in the world to make a bow backwards as it were and if you tied a knot it would be bound to get so tight during wear that you couldn't get it undone.

So the idea of tying it was abandoned and Otto decided that it should be hooked in some way. But he knew that hooking it would not be easy unless it had some sort of give and this would require some elastic being incorporated. This was an additionally good idea because Swanhilda had complained of the rather tight and unyielding feeling on her body. The elastic would overcome that drawback too.

He had not brought any with him but she helpfully rolled off a rubber band from around some of her music and he improvised by pinning that to the two back straps.

'Now let's see how that is,' said Otto. 'Test it. Shoulders up, arms back, thrust out your chest.'

With a KAFITTT! the back straps catapulted apart, bringing home to Otto the fact that the pounds pressure per square inch of a stressed bust can be really phenomenal, especially when you are working in terms of the magnitude of Swan's upperworks.

'Don't worry,' he said, as she regrouped her top hamper into the halter and pulled the back straps up together. 'It will be all right when I use proper elastic. Or better still! I've just thought. Why don't I let in some elastic in each side under the armpits? That way we'll be doubly taking the strain.'

And so, by trial and error, he gradually got it right, and it could be said that on that night in Swanhilda's room in a New York rooming house in 1912 Otto Titzling invented the brassiere as we know it today.

But just as so many other inventors have not realised at the time the ramifications of what they have hit upon, Otto was not aware right there and then that he was at the forefront of a revolution in women's underwear. In point of fact at the moment he took the garment from Swan and knew that he could now make it up into a satisfactory product, his mind was switched to something more personal.

'Now that you're happy with that, and I think it's wonderful, too,' said Swanhilda, 'would you like some coffee?'

And almost before he could say a word the coffee was on, she had cranked up the handle of the victrola and Caruso was rolling out.

Clearly things were designed to be taken at a more leisurely pace than the other frenzied affair but, despite her good intentions, once Swanhilda was on the divan and the top deck was bared she seemed quite unable to keep in rein the emotions he stirred in her. He was to learn that she was wearing fewer of the undertrappings of the previous occasion. As he struggled to respond, suddenly her body went limp and she turned her head away.

'What's wrong?' he asked.

She slowly shook her head.

'What's the matter?'

She looked at him and smiled rather sadly. 'It's no good, is it?'

she said. 'You're not really interested. I can tell.'

'No, it's not that.'

'Yes, it is,' she said quietly, putting an arm through one of the shoulder straps of her chemise and starting to replace it.

This was even worse. Otto felt terrible. He tried to say he felt sorry.

'It doesn't matter,' she said. And then she added, almost to herself. 'I guess I've made rather a fool of myself.'

('Oh, God, this is awful.')

He didn't know what to say to her. He went dejectedly to the door with her and she squeezed his hand as they got there. She smiled at him and said : 'Good night, Otto.'

He took her in his arms and kissed her. She was crying.

He walked to his room feeling as low as he could ever remember feeling.

At the factory next day he made up the finished garment and when he presented it to her that evening nothing was said about what had happened the night before. She seemed quite the way she always had been. He had been dreading their coming together again, but as she examined his handiwork and complimented him on how beautifully it was made ('One of the machinists at the factory, I've got her to thank for that,' he said), she paused for a moment. She looked directly at him and smiled, giving a little movement of her head, just an indication that it was all water under the bridge as far as she was concerned.

What a wonderful girl she was. He felt so warm towards her.

His creation turned out to be a great success. Her friends and associates could not help but notice the change in her appearance and Otto was happy that she was pleased about this. After a week or so of her 'wear-testing' it, as it would be called today, he was in her room and she took her blouse off and he had a thorough look at it, discussing with her how it was standing up to day-to-day wear. Only the shoulder straps seemed to be not quite satisfactory. He decided it would be a good plan to make them adjustable and he told her that he would work out that modification and incorporate it.

As he was looking intently at her bosom and then reached out a hand to ensure that one side of it was fitting properly, she laughed and gave him a gentle cuff on the side of the head. He was momentarily surprised at this and then, realising the significance, he laughed too and on this friendly platonic footing they continued their relationship henceforth.

Girls whom Swanhilda knew who were of similar build asked her where she had got her 'chest halter', as it was called then for want of another name, and she was to come to Otto and ask him whether he could make one for them too. He did this, to their great satisfaction, and soon by word of mouth numerous requests were coming to him.

It would be nice to be able to say that demand grew and that soon he was doing nothing else but making 'chest halters', that eventually he had to hire people to help him and set himself up in business, so that from this small beginning the whole brassiere industry arose. But in point of fact this was not the case.

When he had made quite a number of them, charging merely a nominal price for his time and materials, he had a chat with his Uncle Louie about the business potential of his brainchild. The hardheaded Louie Framer, however, was not very enthusiastic. To his way of thinking it was merely fringe trade, catering to outsize types for whom the conventional corset was not the answer. You could never hope to get the same sort of turnover and return for investment as from concentrating on the mass sales to women of average proportions. His reactionary attitude put a damper on Otto's thoughts of having come up with a wonderful money-spinner.

The outbreak of war in Europe was also to have a bearing on the matter. With the mobilisation of troops in the States in anticipation of eventual involvement, government contracts were handed out by the score for everything from the manufacture of heavy artillery to puttees. Framer went to Washington and came back with a hefty contract for woollen combinations for the doughboys in the wintry months of war. Much of his production was at once switched to this, and anything like the idea of producing a chest halter for big-busted women was peanuts by comparison.

So Otto's revolutionary new item of women's underwear was put aside and, like many another invention, was to lie dormant for years. These things are a matter of timing. The right time for the brassiere to catch on was yet to come, as we shall see in the next chapter, when events in the field of foundation-wear took a turn which necessitated women of all types having such a garment.

Otto shelved his brainchild, not even bothering to patent it, a lapse on his part which, although he was to have no way of knowing it at the time, was to have very unfortunate consequences for him in the future, namely in the form of the arrival on the scene of Philippe de Brassière.

Before leaving the subject of Titzling's rooming house days we should mention what eventuated as regards the one who, after all, had been the catalyst in his evolving the bra – Swanhilda.

One day she came to him with her wonderful news. She had been hired by a touring company that was taking opera across the country right out to the coast and back and the thrilling thing was that it was not just as a Rhine Maiden belting it out in the background; she'd been given a part – a small part, granted, but a part never-theless – in each of the three operas they were doing.

And raising herself to her full height and placing a hand on her bosom she added : 'And, Otto, I owe it all to you, to this halter you made me.'

'Nonsense. It's because you've got a good voice. I'm so glad for you.'

'No, it's thanks to you. I caught the producer's eye, no doubt about that.'

She was away for three months and this, with a holiday she took after the tour with her family in Minneapolis, meant that Otto did not see her again for some time. He had moved from the rooming house and she lived in another part of New York on her return, so that they rather lost touch. When they did meet up again she was married – to the producer – and at length she was to take an early retirement (the producer and she herself knew that her voice wasn't all that good) and settle down in Yonkers, happily rearing what was eventually to be a family of four strapping youngsters.

For his part, Otto married Martha Medina, not before a lengthy wooing of her. Bernard Shaw once said : 'There is only one thing worse than losing your heart's desire, and that is gaining it.' And this could never have been more true than in Otto's case.

Martha was very pretty. She had a beautifully proportioned, trim figure and such an exquisite face that she made heads turn wherever she went. She was vivacious and at a party always seemed to be the focal point. She had always had a coterie of young men around her, whom she played tantalizingly one against the other. Frustration among the men, far from dampening their zest for the fray, made them even more ardent, and the sensitive Otto suffered mightily in this game of rebuffs and minor conquests, and disinterest interspersed with warm affection, which was part and parcel of being in love with Martha Medina.

It was not until he was established and showing every sign of doing well for himself that there were definite signs of his being the front-runner among those who sought her. He did not mind that this was so, since it showed common sense on her part not to want to get tied up with someone who was a born loser. But what he didn't realise at the time was that as the years elapsed more than a few of the aspiring young men she had had on a string had grown tired of what one of them bluntly described as her 'dangling of the carrot' and they had withdrawn from the race to settle elsewhere for someone with whom they knew where they stood. Thus made aware of this drawback to her approach to things and all too conscious of the fact that her thirtieth birthday was coming up, Martha consented to marry Otto.

His friends told him that he was a fool, that she was vain and self-centred and that it could not possibly be a happy marriage. But

Otto, with his feeling of conquest and the sense of pride at having anyone as beautiful as Martha for his wife, could not be made to see this. And in his years of marriage he remained proud of how attractive she looked, how well dressed she was whenever they were out (even if at considerable cost to him) and how men never ceased to take note of her. Keeping her figure was, however, at the expense of not having children, although the way she told it to Otto was that the doctor advised her strongly against her taking the risk of having a child. He deeply regretted not having youngsters and this, coupled with how demanding she was, made him feel more than once that perhaps the marriage had been a mistake, and being resigned to it and getting on with his work was no real compensation.

In later years he saw Swanhilda occasionally and each time she seemed even happier about life with her brood. They would have lunch together when she happened to be in town and talk about old times at the Riley rooming house. And more than once, coming away from a lunch with her, he would think about having married her instead and then do his best to dismiss it from his mind and think about other things.

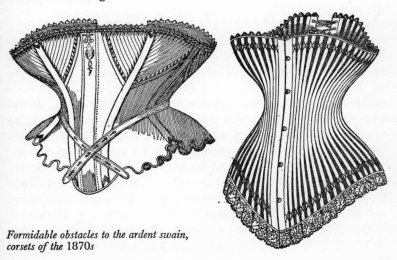

Formidable obstacles to the ardent swain, corsets of the 1870s

The corset, 2000 B.C.; for added decoration, the breasts were left bare

3

A Short History of Corsetry

To show where Otto Titzling fits into the broad picture of women's underwear, it will be helpful briefly to outline its development over the years.

The whole story of the brassiere lies within this century. It did not exist in previous centuries simply because there was no reason for it to exist. Back through time the basic undergarment worn by women to improve the appearance of their figures was the corset, a venerable garment dating back to the Minoan Age, about 2000 B.C. And the length of the corset was such that it could perform the twin task of giving women their desired slim waist and supporting the bust.

But as worn in Minoan times it was not underwear. Usually of richly ornamented leather, it was worn as an outside piece of attire, extending from the hips to just under the bosom, which it pushed up, firmly held out and exposed. However, the fashion for women to girdle their bodies thus, whether visibly or as underwear, did not hold uninterrupted reign from those far-off days until recent years. The ancient Romans and Greeks favoured draped, as against fitted, garments, as is evident from the long flowing togas and tunics of their statues. The wearing of clothing in the mellow Mediterranean regions did not come into being from a necessity to keep the cold out, nor from a sense of modesty. As Cecil Saint-Laurent points out in *A History of Ladies' Underwear** : 'Athenians knew nothing of the eastern Hebrew and Christian beliefs we have inherited which impose the idea that certain parts of the body are shameful. The Greeks did not cover themselves out of sexual morality, but out of love of civilisation. The ardent city dwellers wanted to distinguish themselves from the barbarians.' With the Greeks, as with the Romans, the wearing of clothes was an indication of social stature. Those of high breeding and the well-to-do let it be known that they were such by the costumes they wore, in contrast to those on the lower rungs of society, who went naked.

Underwear as such was unknown, although women might wear two tunics, one of which became a chemise. 'Transparent clothes,' writes Saint-Laurent, 'were all the rage; both garments would be transparent, or just one, in which case it was usually the outer one, contrary to present day fashion. The transparent effect was also obtained with dresses of fine net, which were very revealing indeed. Was there any sense of modesty at this time? It certainly did not apply to the breasts, which many dresses left uncovered, upper class women wearing clothes to show their status, not to hide their physical charms.' Among the ungarbed male peasants, this often gave rise to *erectus publicus*, but in the case of the upper class males, in their togas, it was *erectus privatus*, as indicated in wall drawings still to be seen in Pompeii.

With their conquests in Europe the Romans' influence spread in everything from road and bridge building to baths and even to ball

* Saint-Laurent, C.: *A History of Ladies' Underwear* (Michael Joseph, 1968).

games that were the precursors of modern football. And naturally they influenced the garb of those in the lands they occupied and their preference for softly draped clothes was to persist right through the Middle Ages. The earliest written reference to corsets was in the household accounts book of Eleanor, Countess of Leicester, who entered an item on May 25, 1265 : 'For 9 ells, Paris measure for summer robes, corsets and cloaks.' But it was not until the 1500s that the desire of women to encase themselves in such tight-fitting undergarments became the general thing. By the time of the late Elizabethan era women were really suffering for fashion in the corsets of whalebone and leather, rigid and inflexible, that they wore in imitation of their Queen.

The Puritan influence saw a return for a while to the softer draped

Changing shape of fashion: after the early success of Titzling's shape-giving bra (left), the twenties progressively suppressed the breasts. In the thirties, however (far right), the bosom made a comeback

lines and they of course put a stop to all that nonsense of bosom interest. Puritan women did wear a corset under their all-concealing, unostentatious clothes, but only to keep their backs stiff and erect. They did not have sufficient influence, however, to stop the introduction of the farthingale, or hooped skirt, from Spain and were scandalised at the sort of leg show that could result from the wearing of this sometimes uncontrollable item.

Those who write the history of clothing, that never-ending book subject, tend to smack their lips when they come to the early seventeenth century. The farthingale, with the embarrassment it could cause women caught in a high wind, had gone out of fashion. Now wearing voluminous, relatively close-fitting skirts, women felt they could dispense with wearing drawers underneath. Riding was a

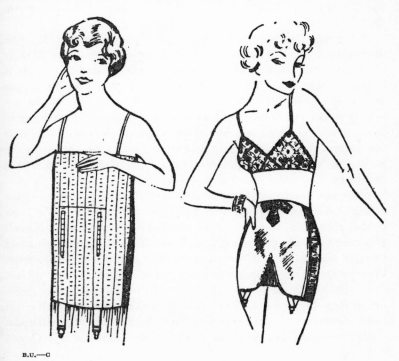

popular diversion with well-to-do ladies and the costume historians never failed to devote space to the hazards of falling from their horses, apart from hurting themselves. To quote Saint-Laurent, 'many writers became infatuated with the subject' and from all the attention it has been given over the years one gets the impression that without such things as movies or football matches to go to at the week-end it did at least provide something to do for young men at a loose end. This sort of exchange :

'What'll we do this afternoon?'

'Let's go and watch women falling off horses.'

'Oh, I dunno. We do that every weekend. Let's try and think of something different.'

At best it must have been a fleeting pastime, and its objective like the point of a shaggy dog story. Either you see it at once or you don't see it at all.

The figure was heavily corseted in this period, in keeping with the female desire to have a shapely form on which to drape all their finery, but the French Revolution put an abrupt stop to this. As it was succinctly put : 'To look affluent was to find yourself on the way to the guillotine.'

Simple straight dresses, with only a chemise worn beneath them, and the avoidance of any sort of ostentation, were the life-saving vogues among French women; and since Paris, even then, was the pace-setter as regards feminine fashions, in England and elsewhere in Europe this trend was followed.

When the Terror was over, women continued to do without tight-fitting underwear and they felt that it was safe now to make their clothes more showy. Literally showy. Napoleon considered himself an emperor in the true classical style and decked himself, his court and his palaces with Greek and Roman outfits and furnishings. Women accordingly turned to the flowing, draped garb of ancient times. But with a difference : they wore high-waisted gowns of gauze which they dampened to cling to the figure. The eye-catching effect was undeniable; the drawback was the high incidence of pneumonia.

By Victorian times the good old corset was back, the dear Queen being the epitome of the strait-laced female, and as the 1800s were drawing to a close the wasp waist was the *sine qua non* of the woman of fashion.

At the beginning of the 1900s the hour-glass figure had become the ideal towards which all women strove, and suffered mightily in the striving. The same ideal was also to be realised in the shape of the Coca-Cola bottle. When the Coca-Cola company asked Raymond Loewy to design a distinctive bottle for them he gave the matter considerable thought before even starting work on it. He observed the obvious enjoyment men drinking after-dinner brandy get from fondling the balloon-shaped glass as they swill the brandy around before taking a sip. Clearly this was symbolism. Subconsciously it was like holding a woman's breast. So why not try to think of something along these lines for Coca-Cola? Result : the bottle with the hour-glass figure. Whether men actually get the vicarious thrill of grasping a woman's slim waist whenever they take a Coke is doubtful, but anyway that was the idea.

In female fashions, however, the hour-glass look referred merely to the front view – the drastically nipped in waist with broad curve of bosom above and wide hips below. The side view was something else again. It was called the S-shape and was among the most unattractive silhouettes women have ever reshaped themselves into. The S, of course, was the outline drawn from the neck out over the bow-window bosom, down across the squeezed-in waist and out around the greatly protruding rump. Bow windows as such had an interesting origin. They came into being in the eighteenth century as a commercial ruse by shopkeepers to make better display use of existing space. But the bow window as applied to women's upperworks didn't make the most of what they had and as we shall see shortly. Otto Titzling's desire to wean women away from this unpleasing frontage brought him disapproval from certain quarters.

It is not always realised that in the old days corsets were not worn next to the skin. They went on over the chemise or other similar type of undergarment. There was a parallel in men's attire. The venerable game of cricket was one of the first in which men wore an athletic support or 'box', to protect the batsman's courting tackle. But at first this was not worn, as today, next to the skin. It was not even worn over the underwear. Like the batting pads and other protective equipment, it was worn outside the player's clothes. At Lord's cricket ground, hallowed headquarters of the game, old engravings may be seen of batsmen taking guard at the wicket with the box securely strapped into position there on their white flannels, which oddly enough did not seem to offend Victorian sensibilities.

The reason it was worn that way was undoubtedly because of the problem of laundering. The way they were made in those days, they weren't the easiest thing in the world to wash and to put a batsman's box through the wringer would of course have been disastrous. Modern materials and the introduction of detergents have solved that problem. Exactly the same thing applied to women's corsets. Containing all those 'steels', the strips of metal used as stiffeners, made them devilish things to wash, so by wearing them not directly in contact with the body, washing was kept down to a minimum. In addition, washing them as seldom as possible was a safeguard against that other corset problem – rust.

One must remember that it was a very metallic garment, with a minimum of eighteen bosom-to-buttock steels, and one can see from copies of the *Drapers' Record* of the 1900s just how much of a bugbear rusty corsets were. This publication aimed primarily at the corset trade was founded in 1887 and it is a measure of how large the corset loomed in the way of life of those days that it could claim to have 'The Largest Circulation of Any Trade Paper in the World'. In the advertisements one could not help but notice what stress the manufacturers put on their claims that their garments wouldn't rust. The attributes of such corsets as the *Fitu* and the *Twilfit* in regard to ensuring the fashionable figure 'For Slenderest Maid, For Stoutest Matron' seemed quite secondary to the blatant heading : 'WILL NOT RUST ! ! !' There were dozens of ads for 'Women's Rust Proof Corsets'. And it was top of the list of the *Apollo's* 'Four-fold Guarantee : 1. Not to Rust, 2. Not to Break, 3. Not to Loose (*sic*) Its Shape, and 4. Not to Tear.'

The man who had overcome this problem for the corset manufacturers was a Mr Brearly of Sheffield. He it was who had evolved stainless steel, in 1912, for the cutlery trade and the corset people were quick to see what a boon it would be for them. In any event they had turned to steel in the first place through its development for other industry.

Originally the stiffeners had been made of wood, horn, ivory or whalebone. 'Bones' were made from the long horny plates set in the upper palate of the whale which had the virtue that they could be split along their entire length of nine to thirteen feet as thinly as desired. Boning was the thing for corsets for many a year but it wasn't cheap, since whalebone came exclusively from the Bay of Biscay, Greenland and the Arctic Circle and required complicated processing. But during the Industrial Revolution, when Bessemer evolved his speedy and economic method of producing steel, it was not only heavy industry that reaped the benefit. Such things as steel nibs came into being to replace the quill pen, which was such a tedious instrument, since it forever needed sharpening with a 'penknife'. And the corsetieres hopped on the bandwagon to adapt this new commodity so much cheaper than whalebone to use as stiffening.

However, as we have seen with the matter of rust, the introduction of 'steels' did not mean that the corset had reached perfection. Though cheaper than bones, they were not as flexible. To try to overcome this and to give the wearer more freedom of movement, a manufacturer introduced a cross-over type of arrangement on the lines of what is done today with stretch fabrics, his being described as 'a patented system of construction, created after long exhaustive tests, in which the Special Double-lever Steels are allowed to slide over one another when subject to strain.' A drawback was that when the woman wearing it became at all energetic it sounded like the Three Musketeers fighting their way out of an ambush. The high metal content of the steel-stiffened corset also presented another hazard, akin to the danger run by golfers with steel-shafted clubs caught out on the course in a thunderstorm – lightning. Having your corsets struck by lightning could be a nasty business.

Although today when we make mention of this old-time garment we refer to it in the singular as a corset, in the days when it was a commonplace it was always called 'a pair of corsets', or as our grandmothers were wont to say, 'a pair of stays'. This was for the simple reason that it came in two pieces, attached in front by a row of hooks on the 'busk' stiffener and united at the back with the notorious lacing, which was pulled as taut as humanly bearable by the good lady's personal maid, husband, female friend or relative or, as has often been depicted, by a mechanical device akin to a fence-wire tightener.

Through association with our grandmothers, we tend not to realise that it was not only the mature woman who wore stays. The dolly girls of that era also wore them since they as much as any of the womenfolk wanted to attain the ideal of the wasp waist, if not more so. The aim in those days was to have your waist the same in inches as your age and you can readily imagine that it took some pretty drastic lacing to achieve a seventeen-, say, or even a nineteen-inch waist. In one passage in his novel *Cakes and Ale* Somerset Maugham gives a good guided tour of what it was like down below a girl's outer clothing and also an insight into a side-effect of the tight corseting : 'She put her arms round my neck and began to cry too, and she kissed my lips and my eyes and my wet cheeks. She undid her bodice and lowered my head till it rested on her bosom. She stroked my smooth face. She rocked me back and forth as though I were a child in her arms. I kissed her breasts and I kissed the white column of her neck; and she slipped out of her bodice and out of her skirt and her petticoats and I held her for a moment by her corseted waist; then she undid it, holding her breath for an instant to enable her to do so, and stood before me in her shift. When I put my hands on her sides I could feel the ribbing of the skin from the pressure of the corsets.'

For Maugham's hero it was all plain sailing, but film actor David Niven has given a good idea of what a real hazard to courtship corsets could be when more than once he has had television viewers rolling with laughter at his description of an incident during his early days as an actor. It appears that he was playing opposite a leading lady long since past her prime but determined, by means of heavy corseting, to maintain the illusion that she had still retained her beautiful figure. The action of the play required him at one point to be clutched to her bosom in a highly emotional, lengthy embrace. Unfortunately, as she swung her arms around his head and brought it down on to her chest, one of the steels of her corset came adrift of its moorings and the end of it shot up into his nose. Unaware of what had happened, she yanked his head back into position on her bosom as he tried to withdraw to free the stiffener from his nostril and with these antics being repeated several times she continued to deliver her highly charged lines, wondering what the devil he was up to digressing from the script and trying to get away from her. The

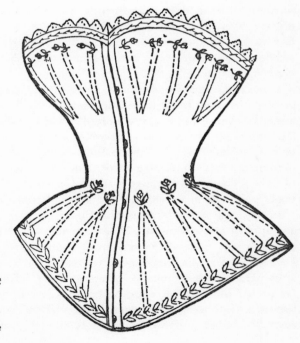

'A real hazard to courtship'. But the heavily-boned corset could do a magnificent job at containing a spreading waistline

audience was convulsed and the lady in question felt so humiliated that she went into long-overdue retirement.

In view of all those steels the corset in the old days did have its uses in courtship as a very effective weapon of defence. If a session on the *chaise-longue* in the parlour got a bit out of hand for the young lady concerned and the point had been reached where it was a matter of 'Without further undo, you can go!' she could always fetch her young man a crack on the nut with her rolled-up corsets. This invariably got the message across.

The nude shows of the Folies Bergère and other Paris music halls were said to have originated 'through the obsession to which men were driven because of the excessive number of clothes women wore'. Paris long predated the major cities of other countries in such licence on the public stage, but we tend to think of the striptease show of today, with its modern titles such as 'Stand By For Take-off', as a comparatively modern American innovation in the theatre, with the famous Minsky's of the 1930s setting the pace. However, in Paris, striptease, as against the conventional nude show, was already booming in the 1880s.

It was called *coucher*–bedtime–and centred around *mademoiselle* getting undressed to go to bed or related activities. It was done in everyday clothes and the very multiplicity of garments of those days that the performer had to get through – dress, petticoats, chemise, corsets, pantaloons, etc. – made it a much more protracted and presumably more tantalising affair than the quicker route to nudity of today. There was one artiste at the Casino de Paris in 1893 who really pulled them in with her speciality – 'Hunt the Flea'.

In passing it is worth mentioning that performing in street clothes also applied to the Can-Can. Nowadays although it is a lively dance to watch it is so devoid of any erotic connotations that Mum and Dad and the kiddies too view it without alarm in the film of the same name and on numerous other occasions. That is because it is performed in what has come to be regarded as the conventional theatrical costume of such events. But in point of fact those were the everyday clothes of the women of the 1890s and it was for this reason

Striptease in fin-de-siècle *Paris*

that it created such a scandal when first performed in France, just as it would not make for a family outing today for a batch of young ladies to come straight from an afternoon tea party to take the stage with a flurry of legs and display of their most intimate underwear.

The 1914–18 war was one of the two main things that brought about a radical change in women's underwear. The constrictions of the corset had a hampering effect in the more active life women led in wartime – working as army nurses, driving ambulances and officers' cars, taking over from men on the home front as bus and delivery drivers, working in munitions plants and so on. The average female in those busy times of national stress would have felt prompted to abandon corseting altogether, had it not been for the fact that in 1913 there had been developed the other big contribution to the revolution in her undergarments – elasticised material, the forerunner of today's stretch fabrics.

Someone had come up with a process whereby liquid rubber could be extruded in fine rubber threads and these could be woven into cloth that was resilient both across and up and down. Two-way stretch was born!

It was found that this could do the job required of a corset, without the necessity of all the complicated stiffeners of steel or whalebone. At first, in a garment known as a 'maillot', the general style of a corset was followed, in that it extended from the hips right up to the bosom. But in time it was realised that it did not need to be that long. Corsets covered that length for the simple reason that the top of the steels would have dug painfully into the wearer's ribs if they had been shorter. It suddenly dawned on the manufacturers who used the new stretch cloth that it could perform the corset's function of controlling waist and hips as a considerably abbreviated item. And so there was another happy event in the women's underwear world. The girdle was born.

However, as can so often happen, you solve one problem only to create another. What about the poor breasts? The corset had deserted them, given up its secondary chore of supporting them. They were left all alone up there, waving in the breeze.

Another undergarment would have to be developed specially for them. But Titzling had already done that. So now all he had to do was to dust off the prototype of the chest halter he had made for Swanhilda and adapt it not just for those with oversize busts but for every type of woman, for whom it was now an essential.

Otto Titzling, bra maker to the masses, was in business.

'Hunt the flea' was a popular speciality in early striptease

4

The Nature of the Animal

Titzling had no difficulty in getting his company financed. His uncle, unhelpful previously, saw what a good thing he was on to now and whistled up the money for him in no time. But with all that settled, this was not the sort of project in which you at once rushed into manufacture on a big scale. After all, it was a new field entirely. The bust had never before been regarded as something to be separately clothed. Previously it had merely been tucked into the top of some other all-purpose garment such as a shift, chemise or camisole and got what support was offering from corsetry which was primarily designed to cater for other parts of the body. Now for the first time as far as underwear was concerned it was a separate entity. In the designing of hats, say, or gloves or shoes much thought has been given over the years to the special requirements of each item. A shoe designer, for instance, must know the physical characteristics of the foot to ensure that he gets things right as to comfort, health, points of stress and so on. This even applies to the lowly athletic support. Parvo Nakacheker, the Finnish athlete who did much of the pioneer work in developing this, devoted much time to the study of pure anatomy and the special demands of such an item. Likewise Titzling, before investing his capital in the extensive project of manufacturing the wide range of styles necessary for catering to the bust, needed to know the nature of the animal.

Today we are more fortunate than he in that there are available to us in bookshops many works which discuss the matter quite openly, whereas in his more inhibited time his research was more painstaking. In essence, however, these were the sort of things he was required to know.

Women have breasts for two reasons. One function is sexual – a highly erogenous zone designed to arouse the male and to be a focal point of erotic stimulation in the female. The other is maternal –

17th-century decolletage and 20th-century uplift—both equally intended to emphasize the breasts as an erogenous zone?

for the feeding of offspring. And it would seem that breasts do a much better job at the former than the latter.

There is no question of their being efficient as an erogenous zone. Complaints about the sexual attributes of the bust are few. But when it comes to feeding time for junior it is a different matter altogether. For a start, things are not made easier for the poor mite by the fact that there is no uniformity at all about where the nipple is located on the breast. As any keen student can verify, the position of the nipple varies so widely from bust to bust that it would flummox even an expert at 'Spot the Ball' competitions.

But even when this orienteering problem has been overcome the shape of the breast may present more problems. What the baby wants is something long and narrow – like a feeding bottle in fact. Mother's rounded contours, proud of them as she may be, may make it difficult for him to take his nourishment without suffocating through having his nose pressed against all that mammary bulge. These considerations led Desmond Morris, in his runaway best-seller, *The Naked Ape*, to view the human female breast 'as predominantly a sexual signalling device, rather than an expanded milk machine'. But is Morris right in regarding the brassiere too as 'simply a sexual signalling device, padded or inflatable so that it not only reinstates the concealed shape but also enlarges it, imitating in this way the breast-swelling that occurs during sexual arousal'?

More accurately, from Titzling's time to the present women have worn brassieres for two reasons : (a) to give the bust support, and (b) to enhance its attraction. With women in general there seems little doubt that the first reason outweighs the second in importance, since after all it is the day-in-day-out function of the bra. Apart from such women as those of the Bazoomba tribe, described below, they side with Dr Derek Llewellyn-Jones, who stresses how essential it is to wear a brassiere 'to prevent the premature stretching of the fibrous supports in the breast'.* Dr William A. R. Thomson, editor of *The Practitioner* and medical correspondent of *The Times*, states

* Llewellyn-Jones, D., *Everywoman: A Gynaecological Guide for Life* (Faber, 1971).

it simply : 'In the woman with healthy breasts that are within the range of normality for size, the purpose of the bra is to give support.' And he goes on to say of women with a somewhat heavy breast : 'In these cases the sound rule is that a bra must be used that is tight enough to prevent the breast "wobbling" when the woman runs or moves quickly. Such wobbling of movement puts an unnecessary strain on the muscles of the breast and tends to lead to unnecessary sagging in later life.'

The sagging aspect has ever been a matter over which women have greatly concerned themselves. In the July 6, 1970, issue of the magazine *Woman* a contributor designated merely as 'Our Endocrinologist' wrote : 'A bra should be worn as soon as the bosom starts to develop. Breasts are composed of fat and glandular tissue, have no muscle of their own. They are supported by the pectoral muscles but without extra support will start to sag and lose their firmness.'

Although this was great publicity for a brassiere manufacturer, it is not strictly true, as evidenced in that little-known work by Mrs Emma Trussitt, *Letters of a Missionary's Wife*, published in about 1901.

With her husband, Ralph, Mrs Trussitt worked for seven years in Central Africa and the book was made up of a selection from her copious letters to a sister in Cheltenham. Much of the Trussitts' time was spent with a primitive tribe known as the Bazoombas. Members of the tribe were at pains to keep the lower parts of their bodies strictly covered, not through any sense of modesty but simply because they felt that if the evil spirits were going to wreak havoc upon them, that was where they were most vulnerable. The upper parts of their bodies, however, were at all times left uncovered.

Mrs Trussitt expressed herself as very distressed about this, particularly as the females of the tribe were described by her as being of 'extraordinary proportions'. Being a Victorian lady, she naturally could not bring herself to go into details, but reading between the lines one can get a fair idea of just how prodigious were the females of the Bazoomba tribe. She wrote of their 'blatant shamelessness'.

There is reference to her having to stop her servant girls from proffering trays of melons to her guests, though she doesn't explain why. Also in one of her letters there is a passage about her husband : 'I'm afraid dear Ralph has not been at his best over the past few days, not his usual dynamic self. Last night he said to me, "I have come out here to do God's work, but I can't concentrate." I'm sure it's the heat.'

An engraving in an early issue of *Illustrated London News* (Some Beauties of the African Jungle) confirms Mrs Trussitt's assessment. And this gives the lie to *Woman* magazine's endocrinologist. It *is* possible for a woman to have firm, upstanding breasts without the help of a brassiere or other support.

In fairness to the anonymous medical man, however, it should be pointed out that Mrs Trussitt made mention of the fact that the Bazoombas regularly rubbed their bodies with oil, which was not without its after-effects. Later research has revealed that this oil, extracted from the root of *Salix jumponna* (the Central African pussy willow) secretes female hormones (the extract is used today in numerous cosmetic preparations on the market) and the application of this oil was a definite stimulant to the development of heightened female characteristics. Unfortunately, however, the males of the Bazoomba tribe, being ignorant of the qualities the extract possessed, also applied it to their bodies, as part of their semi-religious tribal rites. The results, as Mrs Trussitt pointed out, were disastrous, although the Bazoomba men were not aware of what was literally the root cause of their being the least warlike tribesmen in Central Africa. There is no record of their having put up a good fight against any other tribe in the region. The result was that the Bazoombas became woman-dominated.

With breasts to be seen at every turn, Mrs Trussitt set out to do something about it. But her motives were not those of a corsetiere like Titzling coming to the support of womenfolk. With the missionary's oddly warped view that what God has made is obscene, her aim purely and simply was to 'cover up their shame'. She approached the woman she felt best suited to help her in this – Jutti

M'Bwana, titular head of the tribe.

'But,' she reports, 'Jutti just laughed, exposing her big, perfectly formed teeth in a broad grin. However, I determined that something would be done about the situation, with or without her co-operation. I wrote to the Central Office of Overseas Missions, asking them to send me a gross of bust bodices, with which the girls of the tribe could decently conceal from view the upper portions of their anatomy. I specified that I wanted them flesh-coloured, and what do you think they did? They sent me black ones! Oh, the stupidity of Central Office.'

The layman does not generally realise that it is rare for women's breasts to be each of the same size. Titzling, however, was soon to become as aware of this as a tailor is that in men one shoulder invariably hangs differently from the other. When the scope of his business broadened into his dealing with a great number of women he was to find that it was not at all uncommon for his fitters to achieve a nice snug fit on one side of the garment, only to have slackness on the other.

Modern studies have been able to reveal certain explanations for this. The difference can be very pronounced in women continually exercising one side of the body more than the other in work or play, and this was brought out in an article, 'Aspects of Muscular Development of Women in Sport and Industry' (*Medical Journal*, July, 1963). A survey was made of women players on the international tennis circuit who travel the world devoting their entire time to playing tennis day after day at the big tournaments at Wimbledon, Forest Hills, in Australia, etc. It was found that almost without exception that 'the right breast was measurably larger than the left due entirely to the constant exercising of the pectoral muscles by the vigorous wielding of the arm holding the racket both laterally and, more especially, vertically when serving.' A similar situation was found among athletes specialising in such events as throwing the discus and the javelin.

In industry the same thing applied to women incessantly using the right arm more than the left over a period of years in, say, working the lever of a die-stamping machine or operating a loom in a textile factory. The condition was also noted in typists, although in this case it was the left breast rather than the right that underwent enlargement. This was accounted for by the fact that it is with the left hand that a stenographer swings the typewriter carriage back into position at the completion of a line. Interesting figures were produced to show that in a normal day's work a copy-typist on average pulls the carriage across no fewer than 1,200 times. It would take merely a little over three years before such a typist in steady work would have activated the left arm in that way more than 1,000,000 times and 'this sustained exercising of the muscles contiguent to the left breast cannot help but have the effect of enlarging it and giving it added firmness, making it perceptibly different from the other side of the bosom, not similarly conditioned by this factor.'

Like Kleenex, Kodak, Coca-Cola and others, Titzling enjoyed the great commercial advantage of being first in the field.

Previously there *had* been examples of women in various parts of the world taking to the wearing of what was to all intents and purposes a brassiere, but merely in special circumstances, not as a permanent divergence from the rigidly corseted fashions of their usual attire. Such an example is provided by the girls of the wine growing district of Nippoli Grandi, on the Adriatic coast of Italy.

Bobbing up and down in the huge vats, the black-eyed grape-crushers of Nippoli Grandi were in need of some sort of constraining garment for the upper part of the body. Thus came into being what became known as a *flatina*, which in effect was a brassiere.

It is to be seen in a canvas by Toulouse-Lautrec, done when he was on a painting tour of Italy in 1893 – '*La Fille aux Chausettes Pourpres*' (The Girl in the Purple Stockings), which is of course an allusion to the fact that the legs of the girls who trod grapes became stained deep red (except in the areas producing white wines). In the painting the girl is shown donning her *flatina* before starting her day's work in the vats and it is seen to be of white, with wide shoulder straps and a large button for back-pinning.

One can be sure that in those days before the development of elasticised materials it was an extremely uncomfortable piece of apparel. But its function was not to provide comfort for the wearer or to enhance her appearance. It was merely a precautionary garment, brought into being through the necessity of the type of work engaged in, as with the waterproof bloomers of the rice pickers of northern Indo-China.

Such a thing had no commercial value as far as women in general were concerned and could not figure as a rival to Titzling's product. He had a head start on everybody else and by rights things should have been booming for him from the outset. The trouble was that though he had the ideas and the ability to carry them through he did not necessarily have the business acumen to think big and make the most of his golden opportunity.

It was fortunate, therefore, that a chance meeting was to bring him into contact with just the sort of men his firm needed.

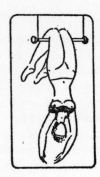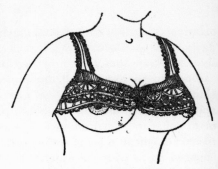

Swing low . . . a bra for trapeze artistes who need other-way-up support

5

Hans Delving

A turning point in Otto Titzling's life was the day he met the man who was to be his life-long associate in business. It was akin to James Watt meeting Boulton . . . Rolls meeting Royce . . . Smith meeting Wesson. Watt invented his steam engine, but he would not necessarily have got very far with it had it not been for his association with Boulton, the man who promoted it and got organisations of all different types interested in using the then new-fangled steam power. Likewise inventive automobile-maker Rolls needed the business acumen of Royce to get the Rolls-Royce really on the road, and gun-maker Smith had Wesson to put the Smith and Wesson revolver on the market in a big way. The man with ideas is not necessarily good at developing them into a workable business proposition. In the case of Titzling and the brassiere it was Hans

46

Delving who stepped in to achieve for it what we would call today 'product acceptance' on a big scale.

On the day the two men were to meet Titzling had dropped into Ben's, around the corner from his factory, for a salt-beef sandwich. He struck it lucky. He had taken a stool at the counter at the precise moment when Ben had set up a fresh side of steaming hot, succulent beef and rather than, as so often can happen, having the disappointment of munching on cooled-off meat, Titzling had enjoyed a salt-beef sandwich as it really should be. So much had it been to his liking that he had ordered another, and it is interesting to reflect that had the sandwich not been so good he would have left right afterwards and not been there when Delving came in. The happy circumstance of their meeting would never have occurred. Truly has it been said that it is strange the part that pure chance plays in our lives . . .

As it turned out Titzling was still there in Ben's when Delving came in, to occupy the stool next to his. Otto didn't mind at all when the newcomer struck up a conversation with him. They talked about topics of the day. Whether Volstead would get his Bill through Congress and dry the country up. The success of this new boy, Babe Ruth. The Great War in Europe that had just ended. 'No, I wasn't in the war,' said Delving. 'I had a physical disability. No guts.' And then he laughed and said that he had been in the services but had not managed to get overseas.

Otto found him amusing. He asked him what line of business he was in and he said : 'I'm sales manager of Baumberger Precision Tools.'

This was not, strictly speaking, true. Delving should have spoken in the past tense. But it was perhaps pardonable on his part not to confess that he was no longer sales manager at Baumberger's, since the break had come only two days previously and the circumstances of his dismissal had been unusual, if not downright unjust.

What had happened was this. Baumberger, although capable of building up a large and successful business, was by nature quite incapable of firing anybody. He could just not bring himself to confront an unwanted employee, face to face, and give him the bullet. When it was necessary to dismiss somebody he would go through tortures evolving some circuitous way to do it. He would get somebody else in the firm to perform the function, or he would write to the person concerned when he was away from the office on holiday, or leave a note on his desk and then stay away for a couple of days until the dismissed one was off the scene. His wife would berate him about his timidity. 'I'm sick and tired of you spending night after night saying, "He's got to go, he's got to go",' she would say to him, 'and then in the morning when you get into the office you don't do anything about it. By the sound of it you've got a bunch of deadbeats there living off you. Are you a man or a mouse? You're the boss. Assert yourself.' It became such an issue in the Baumberger home that he was worked up into a highly nervous state by his wife, who had more than enough of the aggression that he lacked. He was, however, very fond of his wife and liked nothing better than to please her, especially since when he did do something that met with her favour she would, for a period at least, cease her tongue-lashings directed towards him on a variety of topics besides what she felt was his firing aversion. One afternoon at the conclusion of work for the day at Baumberger's there was an office party. Reason for the celebration was that Rosita Dombroffsky, head of the typing pool, had saved up enough of her hard-earned money to have her nose fixed and the result was so spectacularly successful that instead of winding up on the shelf, to which she had become almost resigned, she had managed to snare a husband and was giving up work for married life. The Californian champagne was flowing at Baumberger's that afternoon and even Baumberger himself, who normally was not a drinking man, joined in to the extent of letting his glass be refilled more than once, which doubtless accounted in no small measure for his subsequent behaviour. Hans Delving, for his part, was well away. He had joined the firm just two weeks previously and had been feeling his way tentatively in his new job, since he knew practically nothing about precision tools and had got the job solely by convincing them that it was his ability as a salesman, not his knowledge of the product, that would make him an asset to the firm. As a newcomer in the office, he felt that this party afforded him a good opportunity to get to know everybody better. When the festivities were at their height he strolled over to the boss and in an effort to find out how his stock stood with the powers-that-be he put his arm around his shoulders and said : 'Well, Mr Baumberger, how am I doing?' 'You're fired,' said Baumberger.

At Ben's sandwich counter that day he met Titzling, Delving felt that it was quite unnecessary to get on to the sordid subject of his being momentarily out of work. When you are job-hunting you have no bargaining power with a prospective employer if you announce you're out of work. Much better to infer that you're in a good job but want to change to something you feel would be more worthy of your real talents.

Otto appeared to Delving to be a well-turned-out man with a certain authority about him, the sort of person who might be able to put him on to something. But Delving was to be disappointed when he asked Titzling what his line of country was.

'I'm a meatpacker,' said Titzling.

'Oh, yes?' said Delving, with an abrupt loss of interest. He could not visualise himself in the abattoir atmosphere, with all those carcasses around – and the smell.

But Titzling, of course, had been indulging in the private joke of the corsetry trade. They always said they were in the meatpacking business and to this day it is the stock joke of those dealing in foundationwear. The men, that is. The women in the business tend not to see the humour of it.

'I was only joking,' Titzling said. 'I'm a manufacturer. Women's underwear. I've got my own place around the corner.'

Ah, Delving said to himself, this was something different. Here was a boss, an employer who could give people, like himself, a job. And what a business to be in. It would be wonderful to be able to say, 'I'm high up in women's underwear.'

In no time at all Delving was able to convince Titzling that although his job at Baumberger's was a good one, he was not really happy there. He was looking around for something more congenial . . .

And so it was that the two men came to be associated in business. The chance meeting could not have come at a better time for Titzling. His firm was not actually in financial difficulties, but it was certainly not prospering. Just jogging along. It needed a man with the drive of Hans Delving to put life into it, to make it a really going concern.

Of Delving's talents as a salesman there was no question. He was known as an 'all joking to one side' salesman, a term which came to be commonly used in the trade as applied to the determined type of operator who would just not be put off by anything. It was based on an incident which may or may not have been true but which had always been attributed to Delving. It appears that one day, in the course of his rounds as an encyclopedia salesman he had lugged his case of books up a long flight of stairs, to be confronted when he rung the doorbell by a rugged looking gentleman who did not appear to be an easy prospect. This quickly proved to be so when Delving had only just opened his case and started his spiel and the man exploded : 'For Christ's sake !' He grabbed the case, hurled it down the stairs, the books flying everywhere, and then with a heave he propelled Delving after them. Down on the landing Delving got up, dusted himself off, gathered the books together and returned up the stairs. 'Now,' he said, 'all joking to one side, do you want a set of these encyclopedias or don't you?'

On another occasion, when met with a rebuff not quite as spectacular as the other, merely the succinct verbal advice to 'Scram !', he had murmured as he started to walk away, 'I wish I had fifty customers like you.'

'What did you say !' the man called after him.

'I said I wish I had fifty customers like you.'

'That's an odd thing to say.'

'I mean it,' said Delving. 'Trouble is I've got a hundred customers like you.'

Hans Delving was a great admirer of Elmer Wheeler, the man who dubbed himself America's Super Salesman and wrote books to that effect. Wheeler's approach to salesmanship was : 'Sell the sizzle, not the steak.' This secret of salesmanship was based on Wheeler's observation one day when lunching in an elegant restaurant. Steaks were brought in by the waiters on silver platters, sizzling hot. Wheeler noticed that anyone at a table trying to decide what he would have for lunch, if a waiter went by with one of these sizzling steaks it would invariably make the diner's mind up for him. That sizzle was such a succulent sound that it would make him smack his lips in anticipation. It was the sizzle and the sizzle alone, Wheeler maintained, that sold him on the idea of ordering a steak. So, said Wheeler, a good approach to selling was to do the thing obliquely – sell the sizzle, not the steak.

This was the first of what he came to call his Selling Sentences, and in time firms were to come to him to evolve selling sentences for their products.

A company operating a chain of soda fountains found that customers were reluctant to pay the extra price to have an egg in their milk shakes. They called Elmer Wheeler in and he observed how the men behind the counter went about it. Then he gave his verdict. 'It's all wrong, the way they're doing it. They say to the customer, "Would you like an egg in it?" Automatic sales resistance makes the customer say, "No, thanks." The Selling Sentence for your men is : "Would you like one or two eggs in it?" Without thinking, the customer will say, "Just the one, thank you." And there you have it.'

At another time a group of service stations told Wheeler that they were selling lots of gasoline but had a job getting motorists to buy oil, their sales of which lagged far behind. Wheeler watched their attendants in action and was soon able to say that they were approaching the thing in quite the wrong way. 'When they've filled up the gas,' he said, 'they say to the customer, "Will I check your oil?" The customer at once says, "No, thanks", knowing that he *has* to have gas to make his car go but figuring he can get by a bit longer without buying any more oil. Here's the Selling Sentence they should use. They should look at the guy behind the wheel with a worried look on their face and say : "Is your oil at the right level?" The poor guy visualises his engine suddenly seizing up or some such calamity, and he says, "You'd better check it." And you've made your sale.'

Delving had been very impressed by Wheeler and his Selling Sentences. At all times he had tried to emulate him, and at Titzling's, as we shall see, he was to come up with some very bright ideas, although not all of them were acceptable. As when he had announced to Titzling and the other key men of the firm at a meeting : 'We've got to get into panties. Diversification, I mean. We could produce a real bobby-dazzler and launch it coast-to-coast with the selling sentence – "Not the Best Thing in the World But the Next Thing To it".' 'Oh no, Hans,' Otto had said.

An 18th-century Spanish lady gets buckled in

A nice association was to grow up between the two men both in the office and outside their work. In business they complemented one another perfectly. The more conservative Otto benefited from the get-up-and-go of Hans, and Hans, when he tended to get a bit outlandish, had the checking rein of Otto. 'Now, now, Hans,' Otto would say when his friend showed signs of stepping over the traces. Hans once retorted : 'You'd better be careful, Otto. Everyone's going off to fight the forest fires upstate. If you don't watch out they'll be taking you along as a wet blanket.' But it was all amiable and Hans more than once was able to convince Otto that he should get out of himself, not take his work so seriously, as in the case of their going together to the Brassiere Convention of 1934 at the New Bristol Hotel in Boston, the hi-jinks at which were of such a nature that the management swore that they would 'never have that crowd back again', a decision that was backed to the hilt by the city fathers.

A pioneer in his day, Delving's first bra salesman

6

Man in a Woman's World

At the time when Hans Delving first went to work for Titzling the firm employed women as their sales representatives, which indeed was the common practice in the corsetry trade in the early days. Underwear shops and the equivalent departments in the big stores were naturally a woman's world, as to customers and salesgirls, and of course the store buyers were women. It would have been considered highly indelicate for a *man* to arrive on the scene with his case of samples and start waving around pairs of corsets and other such intimate items in front of the buyer and her all-female staff.

But Delving, then new to the trade and therefore seeing it with fresh eyes, could view it in perspective. To him it seemed all wrong to have women as sales reps.

'We're never really going to get anywhere,' he had said to Titzling,

54

'if we're going to go on trying to get our product across with women doing the selling.'

'It is the customary thing in this business.'

Delving shook his head. 'Women can't sell. If they were any good at selling they'd be out on the road selling everything from canned goods to hardware. Have you ever heard of a Fuller Brush *woman*? Women are no good at selling. A woman couldn't sell a bottle of whisky to an alcoholic. Selling's a man's job.'

Just how far-seeing Delving had been is borne out by the fact that today, with but very few exceptions, all the sales representatives in the brassiere business are men. Probably without realising it, Delving, back in those days before the ramifications of Freud and the sub-conscious had made their full impact, had hit upon a basic psycho-logical aspect of the relationship between the person selling a range of brassieres and the prospective buyer.

A woman-to-woman association across the buyer's desk is not entirely impersonal. The two might talk about how one or the other's new diet is coming along, a terrific new underarm deodorant that you really must try, has little Josie's diaper rash cleared up yet, and other such things that women have interesting chats about. But as regards the marketing of the sample brassieres deposited there on the buyer's desk the interchange is as completely impersonal as a salesman trying to sell a new range of screwdrivers to a hardware merchant.

But now change the relationship to a male brassiere rep across the desk from a woman buyer and the whole thing is on a quite different footing. We all know the basic difference between a man going in to see his bank manager about an overdraft and a woman going in for the same thing. The man's got a tough selling job to do – to get across to that tight-lipped, unconvinced fellow behind the desk that everything's going to be all right, the money will be coming in to wipe it off in no time, etc. But the woman, preceded into the manager's room by a liberal wafting of the scent bought specially for the occasion and dressed to the nines in the form-fitting new suit, sitting down and crossing her legs with a scrape of nylons that could not help but make a man look to see where the noise came from . . . right away it's 'Five hundred? Certainly. But why not make it the round thousand? I think I could see my way clear to accommodating you for that figure . . .' And driving tests. And the difference between a young man at a literary party saying to a publisher, 'It's my first attempt at a novel but I'd like to drop in and have a chat with you about it', and a fetching young lady saying the same thing.

As a writer on human relations in business has described it, it is 'the positive-negative process in action' and naturally the whole chemical reaction is heightened by the visual stimulation of brassieres being bandied back and forth between the two persons concerned. Undertones of sex cannot help but make themselves felt and act to the advantage of the salesman.

And the brassiere firms expect their salesmen to make the most of this. For example, in the salesman's handbook issued by Glamaform Brassieres they list the various steps in selling to store buyers. First the buyer is given the opportunity to see the general appearance of the garment. Details are then given of the types of fabric of which it is made, the workmanship that has gone into it and special features it has to its advantage over other, rival products. Then the important matter of *price*, about which the buyer will ask early on, since if the price is not right for her store there is no point in trying to persevere with the sale. Having established that it is a line in which she could be interested, then comes the vital aspect of 'Displaying the Garment to Best Advantage', and in this regard the handbook gives specific advice :

'The brassiere should be presented lying across the two extended hands, palms upwards, with the fingers in each cup. Each second, or largest, finger should be positioned under the high point of the centre seam and it will be found that with the gentle motion of this and the adjoining fingers the required effect will be achieved, i.e. *make the garment come alive.*'

Glamaform and the other brassiere companies know that there are few women buyers who can fly in the face of Freud and remain unaffected by such symbolism. A woman watching a man put his foot into a shoe, that well-known Freudian example of phallic symbolism, is tame stuff indeed compared to a woman watching a salesman making a couple of brassiere cups come alive.

Of course, the undertones of sex remain nothing more nor less than undertones. Neither the buyer in a large, reputable department store nor the salesman of a leading brassiere company could afford to allow anything irregular to happen during such transactions, since with each personal reputation and the good of the firm is at stake. Brassiere salesmen have to be carefully chosen. 'We do have a proportion of sex maniacs applying for jobs,' as one sales manager put it, 'but they are easily weeded out before any likelihood of trouble may arise.'

In point of fact it is the salesmen and not the female buyers who have to be on their guard. There is a recurring situation as regards small lingerie shops where the owner is the buyer. What can happen is that the woman will say that she likes the look of the garment. And then : 'I'll try it on.' This is the danger signal. She goes off to the fitting room, there's the swish of the curtain being drawn closed and the salesman waits, to the accompaniment of muffled undressing noises from behind the curtain, knowing all too well what will happen next. And sure enough there comes the voice wafting over the top of the partition : 'Yes, it really is lovely . . . but I'm not too sure about the shoulder straps.' He calls over to her : 'You'll see that they have our special "ajusto" fasteners.' 'Oh, yes, I see how they work.' And this Pyramus and Thisbe dialogue can go on for a little while until she eventually hits upon some aspect of the brassiere that requires her to say that she's not quite satisfied with it and : 'You'd better come in a minute.' This is the moment of decision for the salesman. Salesmen have long since found that among women owners of small lingerie shops attractive chicks are few and far between, and – what's more – seldom seem to find it necessary to wear-test the garment before placing an order. So, for the sake of a meagre entry in his order book, is it really worth the ordeal of learning from Mrs Drooper, halfway out of a brassiere, that he's a very attractive young man, etc.?

This is but one of the problems of being a brassiere salesman. There was an incident at Titzling's that has tended to become a recurring occupational hazard as far as the men in the women's world are concerned.

One day Hans went to Otto and said: 'I think you'd better go in and have a talk to Al.'

'What's wrong?'

'He's in bad shape. I think he's cracking up.'

Otto went through to the other room, where the unfortunate salesman was sitting at his desk, slumped forward with his head buried in his arms.

'Hello, there, Al,' said Titzling, kindly. 'What seems to be the trouble?'

Slowly the salesman raised his head and looked up at his boss.

A helping foot . . . modern fittings should be less strenuous

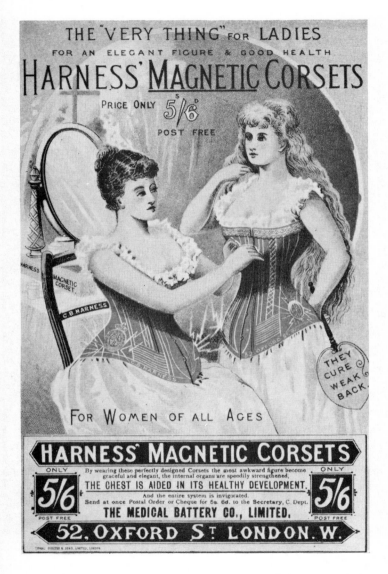

Waisted efforts: the heavily laced corsets of the turn of the
century achieved the fashionable 'hourglass' look.

[face page 58]

Worn over the chemise, the corset helped to push up and shape the bosom from below. But for big-busted girls like Swanhilda, it just didn't go far enough.

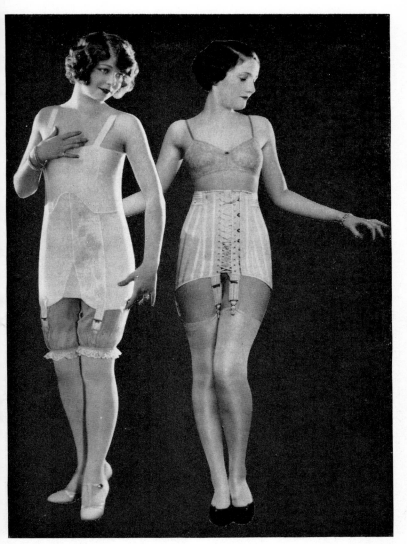

Titzling's pioneering work in creating bras that shaped the bosom was abandoned in favour of the completely uncontoured 'cigarette-girl' look of the twenties (left)—but this in turn gave way to increasingly complex 'shape engineering' in the thirties (right).

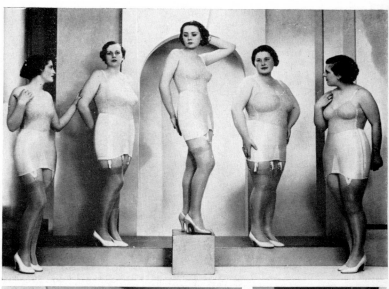

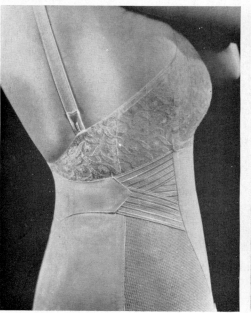

Made famous by Lana Turner, the 'sweater girl' look of the forties was achieved by a bra which turned the breasts into unnatural pointed cones. *Opposite:* 'Miss Treasure Chest 1935' (top): a display of the different female figure-types. Winning the battle of the bulge (left)—power elastic under the arms. Nothing new in see-through (right): today's grandmas knew all about it in the thirties.

Flying high—but wired bras like this are a headache for airport security men. The wiring shows up on their screening machines designed to catch out gun-toting hijackers.

As the sixties went out, the soft natural look was coming in.

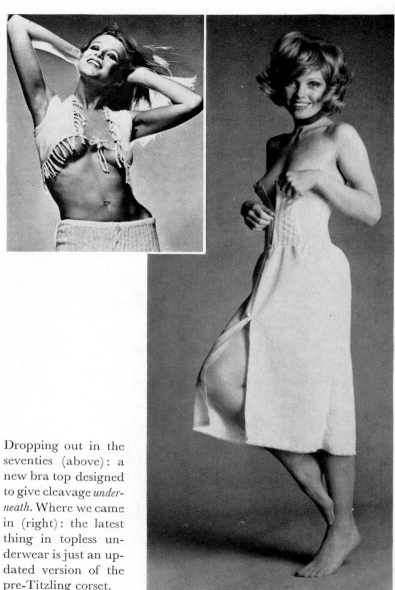

Dropping out in the seventies (above): a new bra top designed to give cleavage *underneath*. Where we came in (right): the latest thing in topless underwear is just an updated version of the pre-Titzling corset.

'Tits,' he said.

'What?'

'Tits!' Al burst out. 'If I see another tit I'm going to go crazy!'

'Now, take it easy.'

'Day after day, nothing but tits! Morning, noon and night.'

Titzling put his arm gently on the salesman's shoulder. 'Come on now, Al. You're just a bit overworked. Why don't you take a couple of days off? You'll be all right.'

'No, it's no good,' he said, obviously under stress. 'So I take a couple of days off. But then I've got to come back to tits, tits, tits, all day long.'

After Otto had chatted considerately to him for a while he went back and rejoined Hans.

'You're right. He *is* in bad shape. I've sent him home and told him to take some time off, as long as he likes until he gets himself straightened out.'

'That's good of you.'

'Least I could do. He's on the point of a breakdown. The reason I knew this – you know what he said?'

'No?'

'He said, shouted almost, "I want a transfer to the jockstrap division." And you know as well as I do that we don't have a jockstrap division.'

Another hazard lies in the fact that men out on the road selling brassieres naturally always have a batch of their products along with them.

On one occasion a salesman had driven home with the back of his car piled up with stock, ready to set off next morning on his rounds. During the night his car was stolen and apart from the annoyance of this he was concerned about the hundreds of dollars' worth of his firm's stock that was in it. The police recovered his car and when he went to collect it the sergeant, not knowing that it had been loaded with merchandise, said that everything seemed to be in order. 'Your logbook's there all right, your maps, gloves and every-thing.' And then, when the salesman was about to point out that all was not in order, to the extent of all his stock being stolen, the sergeant added : 'These were on the back seat. Your girl friend will probably be wondering where they got to.' From his desk he took a bra and a pair of panties, holding them up for a good laugh for all his colleagues. And the salesman, before going on to explain every-thing, realised that it had been a thief with a sense of humour.

Another salesman, interviewed in the course of research for this book, told of rushing through Grand Central Station on his way to catch a train to make a call on a client and bumping his sample case up against a porter's trolley. The catch flew open and his entire stock of brassieres sprayed out all over the floor of the lobby.

'You can imagine my embarrassment,' he said. 'To me brassieres are nothing more than a product I live with all day at the office and out around the stores. But standing there in the middle of Grand Central Station, with all those brassieres spilled out around me! People stopping in their tracks to gape, giving each other a sly look and saying, "Ah-ha!" And me scurrying around trying to scoop them up and get them back in my case as quick as I could.

'I got them all collected and then tried to walk off as nonchalant as I could to my train. But it didn't end there. I felt a hand on my arm and there was a guy up beside me telling me I'd better come along with him. A goddam station dick, I said to myself; now I've got to go through the whole rigmarole of explaining that I was in the business, they were my samples. But before I could say anything he cut me off with a shake of the head and a nod towards all the people around. I'd made enough of a scene as it was; he didn't want another public performance. So there was nothing for it but for me to go with him. I could explain easily enough once I got to his office and back it all up by showing him my card and invoices and other stuff I had with the firm's name on it. But then it suddenly occurred to me as we were going along that he might take some convincing. Kinky guys who go in for that sort of thing always make sure to have some plausible excuse ready.

'So there I am, envisaging all sorts of complications, trying to explain my way out of it and nobody believing me, and I've missed my train anyway, and probably lost the account through not keeping the appointment on time. And then I suddenly realise we're out on the street and the fellow's calling a cab. "Where are we going?" I asked him. "To my place," he said. "Wait till you see *my* collection." '

Hans had been quick to adopt Otto's idea of saying he was in the meatpacking business whenever anyone asked him what he did, and this was not merely because he liked the joke. Salesmen today who use it, or its variant, 'I live off the fat of the land', find that there is a practical side to it. When in a group of men and someone asks what line they're in and they specify it, they immediately lay themselves open to chortles from everybody. There's always some wit present who trots out all the stale old quips about 'He's travelling in women's underwear' and so on. The focal point of the witty jests has heard them all before and is thoroughly bored by them. Far better to avoid the tedious performance by just saying he's a meatpacker, a calling guaranteed to arouse no interest whatsoever from anyone newly met. By the same token, if an underwear man tells a woman it's the brassiere business he's in she can be relied upon almost without fail to give him at once details about every item of underwear she is wearing, where bought, for how much and how it is standing up to the general wear and tear. This is strange but true and perhaps the only explanation is that it is akin to the reaction when someone learns that the person he is talking to is a doctor – 'A doctor, eh? Well, doc, perhaps you can tell me why I keep getting this terrible pain down here . . .' It becomes an occupational bore and it is better not to spark off the topic. Unless of course, as Delving used to point out, the lady in question was intriguingly attractive. 'In such a case it's quite different,' he would say. 'Sex rears its lovely head.'

It is essential that underwear salesmen be knowledgeable about what they're selling and it is said that one of the largest manufacturers, in order that their salesmen should know their products at first hand, insists that each new salesman wears one of their girdles for a week before going out on the road. This is an ingenious way of overcoming the problem all underwear salesmen have – extolling the ease with which one can get in and out of the corset, for instance, only for a hard-to-sell buyer coming back at him with 'What do *you* know about it?' Usually the salesman can only say something to the effect that he has watched his wife putting it on and taking it off. But the salesman with a week's experience behind him can deliver the perfect stopper : 'I know because I've been wearing it for a week.'

However, it is difficult to substantiate this. Although often mentioned in the trade, on inquiry one never seems to be able to find out the name of the firm that requires this of their salesmen. It is thought that it is merely based on the fact that the hard-boiled salesmen of one firm did once convince a naïve young newcomer to the trade that their organisation did insist on this stipulation and had a great old time fitting him out in one and then watching him for a week squirming around on his chair at lengthy sales meetings, at other times slipping out of the room to cope with his garment riding up and in all ways suffering agonies until at length he achieved blessed release at the end of the week.

7
False Pretences

It would make a nice little story to be able to write that Otto Titzling's idea of inflated falsies came to him in a flash, perhaps when watching a youngster blow up a pair of water-wings at the seaside, or when doing boat drill in an inflated life-jacket. But the truth of the matter is that they did not stem from any such sudden inspiration. He would have been the first to admit that his invention of the inflated falsie was derivative. He adapted the idea from a patent already in existence. On May 3, 1929, D. J. Kennedy registered Patent No. 324,870 : '*Breast Pads*, for protecting the breasts from injuries resulting from athletic sports.'

The date is significant. It was less than a year after the 1928 Olympics in Oslo when Lois Lung, probably Sweden's greatest female athlete, had been pressing for victory in the women's 400 metres hurdles. With her legs working piston-like as she burnt up the track, she had gone into the final hurdle with her famous crouching take-off and her right knee had come high up to ensure good clearance of that last hurdle. But unfortunately this had not only cost Lois Lung the Gold. When officials dashed to her, writhing on the ground, she was found to have done herself a serious injury.

The Kennedy breast pads had clearly been the outcome of this unhappy misadventure. The specification for his patent reads : 'The garment combines two groups of annular (ring-shaped) rubber tubes of progressively decreasing diameters arranged in conical form and connected to each other so that when the tubes are inflated a connection of air may pass from one breast pad to the other. The two sets of tubes covered with leather.'

These protective bras enjoyed a certain vogue among women athletes in the 1930s. Members of the American women's field hockey team of 1932 wore them. Some of the players in the England women's cricket side wore them in the 1935–6 season – the year after the notorious body-line bowling controversy in the England-Australia Test series. As one of the girls stated : 'When batting, they give

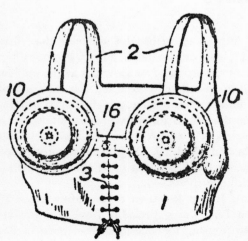

D. J. Kennedy's breast pads, 1929

one just that added confidence, especially when playing forward.'

But the general feeling was that they were an encumbrance, the added bulk far outweighing the advantages of freedom of movement, particularly in the case of a girl already well endowed physically, as with that famous discus thrower Muriel Chesterton (nicknamed, not without good reason, Muriel Chestaton). But a small-busted female athlete had no such problem and in fact found that they served the double purpose of affording protection and improving her silhouette, and it was this aspect that undoubtedly gave Otto the idea of adapting the Kennedy inflated protective bra to a bust-improver for everyday wear.

Previously the standard Titzling bust-improver had been filled with padding and it had been Otto's friend and business associate, Hans Delving, who had come up with their slogan for these : 'What God has forgotten we stuff with cotton'. And it was he, too, who thought up the name for the then revolutionary inflated falsies. It was at the time of Al Smith campaigning for Mayor of New York and the word 'booster', for supporter, was very much in vogue.

'There's our name for them,' said Delving. 'With some sort of slogan like, "What better support can a girl get than Titzling's Boosters !"'

'Boosters' it was, and they were an instant success – not, however, without their shortcomings. Letters of complaints in the Titzling files included such things as a sad letter from a young lady who had bought a new gown to attend her first formal ball and when her very eligible young man had pinned a corsage to it he had gone right through to her Boosters and 'he had been taken quite aback by the sudden outrush of air', not to mention the terrible humiliation suffered by the girl, who naturally saw no more of him and could not for a long time bear to face her friends. Just how they should make amends to the young lady was a subject of debate in the Titzling office. 'Let's just tell her how sorry we are,' said Delving, 'and send her a copy of *Gone With the Wind*.' Otto, however, did not feel that it was a subject for jest and in the end she was put on the free list for any Titzling products she might care to choose.

Inflated falsies were an accepted form of bust improvement for a number of years and they persisted into the 1940s, but still often causing distress to their wearers. There is the true but hitherto unpublished Churchill story of the secretary at the Yalta Conference who was pleased to note that her appearance, which she had augmented with inflated falsies, did not escape the notice of the great man. He could not, in fact, keep his eyes off her. She was crestfallen, however, to realise later when on a visit to the powder room the reason why Churchill was looking at her so much. One of her falsies had slipped. Churchill, with his well-known puckish smile, said afterwards to a colleague : 'I admit I was fascinated – the first three-breasted woman I'd ever seen.'

But that girl's plight was as nothing compared to what was to befall more than one airline stewardess wearing inflated falsies when her plane zoomed up to high altitude. Not only did the sound of exploding falsies cause confusion up front in the pilot's cabin ('Christ ! We're being hijacked !), but, in addition, having a couple of rubber cheaters exploding right there on your chest was downright dangerous to the girls.

The advent of fully pressurised aircraft has now of course removed this hazard, but as it happened the inflated falsie went out of favour of its own accord. The development of latex foam and, later, fibrefill rendered them obsolete.

But the inflated falsie has not entirely disappeared. The Berlei company today admit to equipping their model girls with a modern version so that they go on to the showroom floor filling out adequately each type of brassiere being displayed. Since a big-breasted model cannot squeeze into a small brassiere, it had been found more practical to have only small-bosomed models, who can inflate falsies into the required chest expansion. These latter-day boosters have a self-sealing aperture and the girls blow them up by inserting a drinking straw into the hole and nipping it shut when they have the pressure just right.

It is not given to many – especially not men – to have the enjoyment of seeing half a dozen models in the dressing room standing in a row blowing their breasts up through a straw, while the convenor flurries around them saying, 'For heaven's sake, girls, get your bristols blown up and we can get this show on the road.'

Actually, an underwear fashion show gets funnier. Those who stage such things some time ago decided that having models clad only in underwear walking around striking poses in front of the assembled buyers in the usual style of fashion models was, not to put too fine a point on it, somewhat embarrassing. So – they dance.

But to return to Titzling's time. Not having the benefits of the modern synthetic latex form and fibrefill, the progression from the none too satisfactory inflated bras was to the use of rubber. It was not, however, the complete answer and the reason for this was the difficulty in getting a consistent, stable filler for the built-up bras. To try to overcome this, Titzling evolved a machine for testing the consistency, firmness and resilience of his rubber falsies. Not actually of his own invention, he had developed it from that used in making tests on foam rubber cushions and chair upholstery. When he showed it to Delving, however, he found that he did not share his enthusiasm. 'I may be old fashioned,' said Delving, 'but I can't see the point of all this machinery to see whether they're a natural imitation of the real thing. I'd have thought the best way would be to do it by hand.'

In those days when what were known as 'gay deceivers' were made of rubber, women in general did not realise that the quality of falsies on the market in any given year was directly related to the weather in Malaya. We all know that when we have a wet summer peaches, plums and other such fruit will be big and look good enough but on sampling will be found to be watery. Exactly the same thing applies to rubber, which after all also comes from trees. Whenever they had a particularly rainy season in Malaya, this would make itself evident when the rubber was refined for commercial use. What would be produced is what is called in the trade 'wet rubber'. At such times the rubber that went into falsies was found to be most unreliable. Ideally a rubber falsie should of course be pliant but yet possessing enough 'body' to make it closely akin to a good firm breast. The mild winter and moderately damp spring in Malaya in 1933 resulted in what was regarded as a vintage year for rubber falsies. But a 'wet rubber' season was the despair of the manufacturers, who at best could only produce a product they knew could not be relied upon to keep its shape and at worst confronted them with what was known in the trade as the 'hot water bottle' problem, when the rubber content would break down altogether and give rise to countless complaints from customers about the disconcerting sound effects coming from their chests.

It was this unreliability as far as raw materials were concerned that as much as anything else brought an end to rubber falsies. In any event, the outbreak of war and the cutting off of supplies from Malaya brought a halt to production and after the war the manufacturers never resumed production on anything like the same scale. And by then it was found that, as in many other fields, the new synthetics could do a much better job.

But the irony of it all is that having arrived at a really good natural-seeming padding with latex and its companions, as the 1970s were getting under way the situation had arisen whereby a slump descended on the falsie trade. A sort of Parkinson's Law : At long last get it right and then nobody wants it. Women's Lib and their burning of the bras, plus the influence of the permissive society meant that many females just didn't bother wearing them, whether falsified or not, and this could not help but affect sales figures.

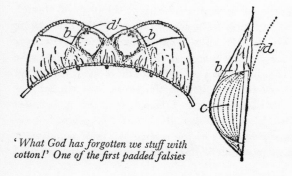

'What God has forgotten we stuff with cotton!' One of the first padded falsies

Titzling's inventiveness knew no bounds. Besides his pioneer work in the field of falsies, he evolved such things as what became known as the bra with the Built-in Mad Money Purse.

This idea came to him when he observed how women, when they didn't appear to have their purse available, would tuck money or keys or some other item of value into their brassieres for safe keeping for the time being. To get a guide as to whether having a built-in change purse would be a practical idea, he mentioned it to one of the older women on his staff whose opinion he valued.

They discussed it for a while, and then she suddenly said : 'I know! Why not a little purse in there for mad money?'

'What's mad money?' Otto asked her.

'You know what mad money is. Anyone who has daughters knows only too well –' She broke off, remembering that he had no children. 'Well, we mothers know. It's money you give your daughter when she's going out on a date. She may have a row with the young man. She gets mad at him for paying too much attention to another girl or he may get objectionable. Anyway, she's mad at him and she wants to leave him flat and come home. She isn't stuck. She's got the money to come home.'

That was good enough for Otto. He had soon evolved a little change purse of light material with a simple fastener that was stitched inside the front of the brassiere at the cleavage. First one off the production line he gave to the woman who had been his adviser for her daughter, enclosing a note of thanks, and this novelty was to prove a big seller.

Another idea he launched was the perfumed bra. Although it was a brainwave on his part to get a textile manufacturer to develop a fabric impregnated with scent, this number was not an unqualified success.

One of the drawbacks was that he got continual complaints from the man who made the cloth for him. His workers were flaking out from the fumes, as they worked over the bleaching vats to which the perfume extract was added, and he had to put them on short shifts and pay them the extra hazard money they demanded. Hans too had his troubles. The simulated perfume used had staying power, which meant that the garment would stand up to innumerable washings without losing its fragrance. But also it had staying power as regards getting on your hands and clothing when you spent any length of time handling batches of the garments, as Hans did. Finally he had to go to Otto and tell him : 'A great idea for the women who wear them. But it's murder as far as I'm concerned. I get hell from my wife when I get home. She will just not be convinced that I reek of scent from working with this new number of ours.' And when Otto smiled, he went on : 'It's no joke. And now there's even worse than my problem with Rita. Do you know what happened today? I'm in the McKinley Building making a call and when I'm coming down in the elevator afterwards the elevator boy – he'd given me a sort of a look when I'd been going up – anyway, on my way down he stops the elevator between floors and starts chatting me up ! Don't laugh. I tell you, you can make this a discontinued line right away as far as I'm concerned.'

8

Opening Gambit

Titzling's development of the front-opening bra was a definite breakthrough. But credit must be shared with the colleague who set his mind thinking on these lines.

One evening, in the course of a visit to the wife of a friend who had gone upstate on business, Hans Delving was watching her struggling to undo the back-pinning of her brassiere when it struck him how foolish it was that women had to go through such frustrating and time-wasting gymnastics to perform the simple operation of undoing their brassieres.

It came to him as a flash of inspiration that the obvious thing to do was to have the opening at the front. This might seem to be an elementary bit of reasoning but it is interesting to note that people will persist with something that is basically not practical for years, for generations, until somebody comes along and suddenly rethinks it. A perfect example of this is men's shirts. From the time men started wearing the modern shirt, from the latter part of the last century, it opened only part of the way down the front and was put on over the head like a nightshirt. Men suffered this inconvenience right up until the 1920s, when a New York shirt manufacturer got the bright idea of having it open all the way down. It at once gained general acceptance in the States, but it was some time before it caught on in Europe, the British male being the most reluctant of all to break with convention, not completely adopting what was called the 'American coat shirt' until after World War II.

Although Hans Delving was of course not to know that all this was to happen in the world of men's shirts, his brassiere idea was the same simple revolutionary break with convention.

When he got into the office after having his brainwave he said nothing at first to Otto about it. Acting on the sound principle of salesmanship that the way to get an idea across is to present something tangible, he got one of his sample bras and with the help of one of the girls on the machines remade it so that it opened in front. He got Miss Wasserman to model it and with the comment, 'I think we've got a winner here, Otto,' unveiled it.

Otto was impressed. He perfected the rough-and-ready design and some samples were run up. These were wear-tested, although in those days it was not called wear-testing and was not nearly such a thorough process, instead merely being a matter of getting some women to try it for a while and say what they thought of it.

'I'll take a couple for friends of mine,' said Hans, and it was not long before he was able to report : 'Great ! I find it so much simpler.'

'*You* find it so much simpler?' said Otto.

By the time production was under way Hans had come up with the appropriate Selling Sentence. 'This is the way you sell it,' he said, holding it up before his assembled salesmen. 'You say to the buyer, "We call this new number *Sesame*." Then you undo it and say, "See, it opens so easily." '

When *Sesame* had been on the market for a while Hans came

into Otto's office one day and remarked: 'I'll tell you something interesting I've found out about it when I've been out and about.'

'What's that?'

'You and I call it a front-opening bra. That's what men call it. But women call it a front-*fastening* bra.' He laughed. 'A basic difference of attitude. The old battle of the sexes.'

But whatever it was called, *Sesame* and other versions of the same type that they produced did not live up to the great expectations they had had for it. It was not a winner and it most certainly did not repeat the revolution that had been brought about in menswear with the introduction of the coat-shirt.

Although the advantages of the front-opening bra seemed obvious to Hans Delving, it did not meet with ready acceptance from women. There were several reasons for this, objections which were primarily feminine and which would not occur to men.

In the first place, having the fastener in front could mean that it would 'spoil the line'. In a tight-fitting sweater, for example, or a dress of light material the outline of the fastener underneath could protrude unattractively and mar the smooth lines of the frontage.

Also, fastening the bra in front cut right across the rules laid down by brassiere fitters in the stores as to the correct way to don the garment. Men, who have far more interest in women getting undressed than getting dressed, have rarely bothered to observe how a girl schooled in the proper technique for putting a bra on performs the operation. As the *Fitter's Handbook* of the Foundationwear Guild points out on page 51: 'The customer should lean forward as the brassiere is put on and joggle the breasts so that they fall easily and naturally into position in the cups before it is fastened. Then stand up and give the brassiere a firm pull down at the back until it is low enough to anchor under her shoulder-blades. The shoulder straps should be adjusted so that they give a firm but comfortable uplift to the bust, but without pulling the back of the brassiere up and away from its anchorage under the shoulder-blades.'

The key to the whole thing, as any fitter will tell you, is the joggling of the breasts into the right position, which in simple terms

is akin to shaking a pillow to get even distribution of the down inside
If this essential preliminary is not done it can result in uncomfortable
bunching or high-riding, with its unattractive overspill above the
bra, or the unhappy lopsided situation. There is nothing worse than
seeing a girl prodding around to get the even distribution she should
have assured for herself at the outset.

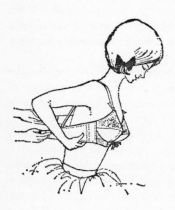

'*Joggling the breasts into the right position*'.
From the Foundationwear Guild's Fitter's
Handbook

With front fastening a woman cannot do this initial manoeuvre
of leaning forward and taking up the slack naturally. The very
action of pulling the two front halves of the brassiere together to
attach them cannot help but result in bunching of the bust.

But these considerations are far outweighed by what is the main,
psychological reason why women do not take to the front-opening
bra. It is a further example of the strange way in which the female
mind works and which men will never be able to fathom.

Women don't like the front-opening brassiere because it doesn't
look good hanging out to dry on the clothes-line.

To a man this would seem quite daft, but consider this. She is
sitting there in the kitchen having a morning coffee and a reverie
about what might transpire in regard to the attractive man who has
just moved in up the road and he works at home – the suburban

housewives' special. And then she happens to look out of the window and sees her newly acquired front-opening bra. Grotesque ! The way it is hanging stretched out there, with one cup over on the left and the other cup to hell and gone over on the right. At least an ordinary bra hanging out to dry follows the normal contours of the figure. But this ! This looks as though she is weirdly deformed.

So, down comes the bra and that's the end of it as far as she's concerned.

Thus it was that *Sesame* came to be a loser in regard to sales. It soon became a discontinued line and even today few manufacturers have such a bra in their catalogues, except of course for nursing mothers.

9

The Big-Busted Woman

Those who knew him well will tell you that it was Otto Titzling who originated what has now, in translation, become a stock joke. He said that 'women's busts come in four basic sizes – small, medium, large and *mein Gott*!'

For women in the *mein Gott* category, if the fact that they can't get their blouses to meet in front were their only worry, things wouldn't be too bad. But that is just one of so many problems both for themselves and for those required to outfit them.

It's not much fun when you're in the fitting room trying desperately to find a good top hamper damper and you overhear a salesgirl saying, 'She doesn't want a bra fitter, she needs a quantity surveyor.'

If she wears anything at all revealing she lays herself open to

76

ribaldry. Like the woman at the rugby dance who felt she would really set things alight in her strapless evening gown, only to have one of the rugger players come over to her and say : 'Excuse me, madam, but I think your dumplings are boiling over.'

Dana Gillespie, who came to fame in the rock musical *Catch My Soul*, epitomises the big bust syndrome.

'I wore my first bra aged twelve,' she will tell you. 'At fourteen I measured 36. Seventeen took me to 40. Now, four years later, I'm up to 44 inches but I think, thank goodness, I've reached my peak.'

She admits that her bust is not without appeal to men and that in show business 'my shape has brought in money when I've needed it.' But it isn't very nice having to put up with feminine reaction. 'I just can't stand the females in the audience who scream with laughter when I come onstage,' she says.

And Dana makes another complaint, one common to all big-busted women : 'When I go to buy a bra in my size I find that manufacturers don't make them in pretty fabrics.'

A basic reason for this, of course, is that making a brassiere for a 44-inch bust is an engineering problem. As Otto Titzling pointed out to his father, the considerations which a bridge-builder has to bear in mind – load capacity, stress, etc. – are always there in the making of any brassiere but naturally it is very much more so when confronted with the really big bust. Therefore the very containing of those giant spheres calls for a more extensive and stronger form of construction than when merely having to deal with a moderately proportioned bust. After all, a footbridge over a stream can be a simple lightweight affair compared to the weighty piers, abutments, interlaced girders and so forth needed for a railway bridge across a canyon. The job the big-bust bra has to do dictates its utilitarian look.

However, modern materials have eased the problem in both spheres. The ponderous construction of the nineteenth century's stone bridges is now no longer necessary, with the development of new materials such as pre-stressed concrete, which can do precisely the same job with a 'wafer thin' bridge. And this has an exact parallel in the matter of brassieres. In our grandmother's time, making a brassiere for a massive-busted woman was really a production, the workmanship that went into it being akin to the skills required of a hammock-maker. But today, with the development of all the new man-made fibres, lightweight materials can be every bit as strong and give just as much support while looking relatively flimsy and, *ergo*, much more feminine.

Even so, the big-busted woman's lot is not a happy one. Manufacturers *can* make bras for them in the delicate, pretty synthetic fabrics they use for women not so expansive. But the majority of them don't do so for the simple reason of their own economics. When putting a new bra on the market they know that they are going to make their killing in the sizes around the 34-inch average. If they include such sizes as 42 and 44 they are merely putting up their over-all production costs for a limited sale in the upper brackets. And they feel that it is just not worth it. The same thing applies in sweaters and countless other garments, but nevertheless it is galling for the big-busted girls to have to look wistfully at a smashing new line of bras in a shop window and know that there is no point in asking for it in their size.

The big bust is a terrible nuisance to female competitive swimmers. It's a drag. Even when confined in the 1920s type of flattening swimsuit worn by such girls, in the case of the big-busted swimmer it has been calculated that it can lose her anything up to 1.7 yards over a 100-yard dash and it is a contributing reason why women's times never approach those of men in swimming events.

When it comes to marathon swimming the slowing-up effect is even more pronounced. In swimming the English Channel, for example, a girl can be ploughing through the water for fifteen hours or more, so that to keep undertow to a minimum she has to keep her breasts severely battened down. And this creates another problem. Having the bathing suit really tight means that in time the shoulder straps bite into the shoulders and since in the course of a

Channel swim the poor girl is going to swing her arms up out of the water 40,000 times or more, this can caused serious chafing. Men, with their flat chests and clad merely in swimming briefs, have no such problems.

In view of this advantage enjoyed by men, some years ago an attractive American marathon swimmer named Lucille Campion announced that she would be making her attempt on the Channel bared to the waist, just like a man. This news was naturally welcomed with enthusiasm by every editor of the popular press and only the fact that it was in the days before the portrayal of female upperworks became permissible in the public prints thot prevented them from giving their readers a frontal preview of the young lady stripped for her Channel swim.

In point of fact it was all a publicity stunt, since in the event she did not take the water as announced, much to the disappointment, incidentally, of a much larger crowd than is usual on the Calais foreshore on such occasions. Miss Campion knew perfectly well that although going topless would give her that greater freedom of movement through the water enjoyed by men, it would be quite offset by the trawling effect of her released bust.

This basic difference of anatomy between female and male

swimmers, with their bodies in suspension as it were, has another interesting aspect. When the author was covering the story of Canadian Marilyn Bell, youngest girl swimmer ever to conquer the Channel, he noticed that the men put into the water to swim beside her as pacers would from time to time drop back, tread water for a while, then swim up to rejoin her. 'Having a rest?' I enquired of her coach. 'No,' he said. 'Having a pee.' And he then explained the interesting fact that whereas it was something a woman could do while continuing to swim, men had to take time out for it. So it would seem that what women lose on the swings they make up on the roundabouts.

Apart from normally large breasts, a glandular upset can cause spectacular enlargement of the bosom. Though the fame of plastic surgeon Sir Archibald McIndoe rests largely on the brilliant work he did on RAF pilots burnt and disfigured during the war, his talent found other outlets as well. There was the ATS girl whose job it had been to drive a Staff officers' car. She had had a glandular upset which had caused her bust to get bigger. And bigger. And bigger. At length a time came when it was quite impossible for her to wedge herself in between the driver's seat and the steering wheel. A visit to McIndoe's East Grinstead hospital, a special application of the surgeon's skill – and all was well.

One of Sir Archibald's last cases before his untimely death concerned the Greek wife of a Turkish army General. She had been a cabaret dancer in Athens and had been billed as 'The Girl with the Perforated Stomach'. Besides being an intriguing publicity line, it happened to be perfectly true. She had been involved in the Greek civil war and had run foul of a sniper with a machine-gun. His burst of fire had gone across her midriff but miraculously she had survived and those Allied soldiers who saw her perform when they were stationed in Athens will confirm what a crowd-puller she was when she went into her exotic dance and displayed the row of bullet scars across her stomach, as advertised outside.

On her marriage to her General she retired to domestic life in Istanbul and, as invariably happens with dancers and athletes when they give up their energetic activities, she began to put on weight. And a big proportion of it she put on up top. Her bust had always been ample and had borne her in good stead during her dancing career, never failing to catch the eye when the novelty of the perforated stomach had worn off. But now, living the easy life, her upperworks had become not far short of enormous.

When she learned that the famous plastic surgeon Sir Archibald McIndoe was on a visit to Turkey, she took the opportunity of consulting him and was pleased to hear that an operation to reduce the size of her bust would be a simple matter. He could do it while he was there in Turkey and she would be out of hospital and home in no time. This fitted in very well. Her husband was away at the time at a military conference in Paris and it would be a pleasant surprise for him on his return to find her figure restored to the attractive proportions it had had in her younger days when he had married her.

She went into hospital and was being prepared for the operation when her husband arrived home. A disagreement among the delegates at his conference had brought it to an abrupt halt before it had really got started. On arrival home the servants told him the

A drastic solution to the problems of the big bust: an iron corset from Renaissance Florence

reason for his wife's absence and he was furious. Nobody was going to perform such an operation on his wife, nobody was going to interfere with what he regarded as far and away his wife's greatest asset. He dashed to the hospital and when those in the lobby tried to constrain him from storming up to the operating theatre he took out his pistol and fired two shots into the wall as fair warning that he meant at all costs to stop the operation. The hint was taken and hurriedly he was ushered up to his wife's room and a stormy scene broke out between him and McIndoe and his wife.

The head of the hospital having been located, he was brought at all speed to the scene of the turmoil and when he got to the door a nurse was coming out.

'It's all quiet now,' she told him. 'The General says he'll let the doctor operate.'

'Oh, good.'

'Provided he makes them bigger.'

The fact that there are a considerable number of men like the Turkish General, if not quite such gluttons, means that it is not all bad news for women with large bosoms. It has been of immeasurable help, as we know, to many a girl with aspirations in Hollywood and elsewhere in the entertainment world. Such a useful counter-balance is it for a girl with slim acting ability that girls such as Jane Russell, in the 1940s, and Raquel Welsh in more recent times were able to achieve international fame before they had even appeared in a film, being in the same category as the well-known Hollywood star of whom it was once said that 'all she has achieved she owes to udders'.

For the girl who wants to put across a really elevated impression, there is the platform bra, which, in the words of Anthony Forge, Professor of Anthropology at the London School of Economics, 'converts the primitive droop into the civilised thrust'. (Showbiz circles, rather more brusquely, term the effect 'jelly on a shelf'.)

One who leaned heavily on such bras was the late Jayne Mansfield, who was able to achieve such spectacular jut by that means that when she was photographed on a sight-seeing tour on her first visit to London a caption writer for one of the papers could not resist the

temptation to put a line over her pic which read : SEEING LONDON
FROM THE TOP OF A BUST.

But not always did she wear the platform type. At the BBC
Television Centre they have one of hers of another style, which the
person in whose possession it is swears she left it there inadvertently
in the course of doing a TV show for them. It is no secret that when
Jayne's bust was in the off-duty position it was very low slung and,
since there was much of it, it wasn't the easiest thing in the world
to get it up and kept there for the famous silhouette she presented
to the world. At the BBC they call it the Jayne Mansfield Hijack
Bra, since it is constructed of the weirdest assortment of slings and
guys to jack things up into place. It is kept in Room 12B on the
second floor and if you ask them nicely they'll let you see it.

As a footnote to the fact that there can be great advantages as well
as problems in this field, it should be mentioned that there is an
English woman who is capable of hatching chicks in the cleavage of
her voluminous bust. This was brought to the attention of the
television-viewing millions by Lord Snowdon in a programme he
produced about people and their odd pets. The woman concerned
was seen to be sitting up in bed in a low-cut nightdress with an egg
between her breasts and nobody quite knew what was coming until
all of a sudden there was a pecking, the shell broke and out popped
a chick. Later the authenticity of this was challenged in a story in
the press, the allegation being that Lord Snowdon had hoaxed the
viewers with some clever cutting whereby a newly hatched chick had
been taken from an incubator and substituted for the egg in the bust.
This was a slur on his integrity and, after all, it would hardly be the
sort of hoax that would be worked on the public by the husband of
the Queen's sister. It did not take into account his great sense
of timing, the wonderful facility of erstwhile photographer Tony
Armstrong-Jones to be in the right place at the right time, which
had made it possible for him to be in the good lady's bedroom, with
the camera focused on her bosom, lights in place, recording machine
in action and all other equipment rolling at the precise moment when
the chick decided to make its entry into the world.

10
Hollywood Interlude

Titzling's call to Hollywood from Apex came in the mid-1930s when the movie capital was in its heyday. Apex Pictures Inc was not one of the major film companies, merely doing well enough producing family movies. They made low-budget westerns, in the making of which they saved a lot of money on location by such expedients as filming the baddies chasing the goodies from left to right across the screen and then getting them to turn around and chase each other from right to left, for their next production. They made movies with child stars of the Shirley Temple type ('Why, Daddy, you're crying!') and hospital dramas ('There's only one man who can save your child's life, madam – and he's in Vienna').

But in the mid-1930s cheesecake became a big money-making commodity in the movie world. The phase of the flat-chested 'boyish' look was over. The feminine ideal was no longer Clara Bow, 'The It

Girl'. Now the public didn't want a girl with It. They wanted a girl with Them. Upperworks became the focal point of the female form divine. Bosomy Mae West was the new symbol. 'Vital statistics', in existence before but not worthy of mention because of the straight-up-and-down look, now became the big thing. 'Pin-ups' came into being and busty young females flocked to Hollywood from all over the nation to try and cash in on this new trend.

Apex Pictures, wedded to their family image, did not at first do anything about climbing on to the busty bandwagon, but at length they came to the decision that they, too, must get into the glamour business.

The biggest box-office attraction they had on their books was Dick Malone, the burly Adonis who starred in their action films. Big Dick Malone had a built-in appeal for every female movie-goer across the nation. But they had no one of commensurate stature under contract as far as feminine stars were concerned. The thing to do would be to try to get Helga Lemurr, the newcomer who had just become the movie sensation in Europe. Big Dick Malone and Helga Lemurr – what a combination that would make.

Helga Lemurr had hit the headlines, not to say scandalised the more sedate elements of the public, with her appearance in a German film called *Auf Wiedersehen*. It had gone on release in Germany and Austria, and in Denmark and the other Scandinavian countries. But Italy and the other Catholic countries had turned it down flat. There was no English title for *Auf Wiedersehen*, for the simple reason that Britain, America and the whole English-speaking bloc had also banned it, on the score of its lurid love scenes. But people in the movie trade had dubbed it *Till We Mate Again*.

The 'lurid love scenes' in *Auf Wiedersehen* were, by modern permissive standards, very tame indeed. But at the time they were considered really something and it is interesting to reflect how movie audiences of those days were conditioned by the Hays Office and the Code of Decency it had laid down for Hollywood. Helga Lemurr and her lover kissed *lying down*. This was sensational to anyone brainwashed by the Hays Office into believing that people who inhabited the silver screen never kissed any way but standing up. This censorship edict was not relaxed until the 1940s, with the making of *From Here to Eternity*, the breakthrough as far as Hollywood was concerned, with Deborah Kerr and Burt Lancaster having their now famous beach kissing session in the shallows – *reclining*. But even at that it was not really a weakening on the part of the Hays Office as far as moral standards were concerned. They merely gave in to pressure from Hollywood big business interests. CinemaScope had just been developed and the movie moguls' argument was : 'How the hell are we going to fill the new wide screen with lovers having to stand up all the time !'

But to return to the 1930s. In addition to what was regarded then as explosive love scenes, *Auf Wiedersehen* also had a nude sequence which was deemed really hot stuff and was the main reason for it doing sell-out business in the countries where it was shown and for it being banned elsewhere. Again, by today's full-frontal standards, it was tame. Helga Lemurr was in the nude all right, there was no question of that. But the director, Wolfgang Ratreis, *l'enfant terrible* of Berlin's Kinemashaften Studios, had shot Helga's nude bathing scenes in the early-morning mists hanging heavy over the Bavarian lakes.

The camera lingered lovingly on Helga undressing on the lakeside, besporting herself in the water and then at length emerging from the lake to take an unconscionable time towelling herself. But so shrouded in mist was the whole operation that the viewer had to draw heavily on his imagination to feel that he was really seeing anything. Some of the less bright citizens of the German hinterland, it was said, went back time and time again to see Helga's nude bathing scene in the hope that the mist would clear.

But even though it was bland in comparison to what we see today, *Auf Wiedersehen* was the sensation of Europe at the time and it made Helga Lemurr overnight the most talked about movie star on the Continent. And as such, of course, she was immediately regarded as a hot property as far as the Hollywood studios were concerned.

It would have been thought that in competition with M-G-M, Paramount, Fox, RKO and the other big boys, Apex would have had little chance of getting Helga. But as has happened more than once before and since, a smaller company can beat out a bigger rival in such matters for reasons not directly concerned with the contract they are trying to get signed. Kinemashaften, who owned Helga, had a link with Apex. They had exclusive European distribution rights of all Apex's westerns, from which with no production outlay on their part they made a great deal of money. This contract was up for renewal and was therefore a stick Apex could wave at them. We'll pay a price that measures up to what the others are offering for her, said Apex, and if you let us have her we'll renew your contract for the westerns.

And thus it was that Apex got Helga Lemurr. She crossed in the *Bremen*, had her legs photographed sitting on the ship's rail in New York harbour and found her way out to the coast with much ballyhoo in a banner-bedecked train. And although financially they had dived in at the deep end to get her and they would have to spend a lot more in promoting her, Apex knew that they had a great investment in Helga, the start of a new era for their company.

And then came calamity.

Helga was found to be not the easiest person in the world to deal with. She was temperamental, given to moodiness. Except for her dresser and her personal maid, whom she had brought with her, she didn't want people around her. She let it be known that she had disapproved of the ballyhoo that had surrounded her arrival in New York and on the train trip and from the outset in Hollywood showed herself unco-operative as far as publicity stunts were concerned.

Apex, of course, wanted to go all out on publicity, and the first stunt had been arranged for the weekend after she got there. Cooked up by the Apex publicity boys, it was as brilliant as it was novel. Helga would go for a swim on Malibu Beach. She would get caught in the surf and in her efforts to get back to the beach she would lose her bathing suit. A friend would dash down to the shallows with a beach towel to cover her embarrassment and by happy coincidence a press photographer would be on that part of the beach at the time to record the event.

But Helga refused to do it and no amount of persuading would change her mind. But what about her nude swim in *Auf Wiedersehen*, she was asked. That was different, she said. That was art. It was an integral part of the plot. This was nothing but publicity of the cheapest sort and she would not stoop to it.

Abe Keppelman, Mr. Big at Apex, was not unnaturally grieved at this refusal on the part of his hot property to play ball with his publicity department, not only in regard to the Malibu stunt but also refusal to pose for pin-ups and other accepted methods of exploiting a sex bomb under seven-year contract. She was a legitimate actress, she said; her reputation would stand or fall on her performance on the screen. Heifer-dust, said Keppelman.

It was suggested that a merit might be made of her very reluctance to get caught up in the general hoopla of Hollywood publicity. She could be built up as a mysterious, withdrawn character, who kept herself to herself. But that idea was thrown out without any need of discussion, since Garbo already had that angle well and truly sewn up.

But this aspect of Helga Lemurr was not really the disaster. It all came to a head when there came to the ears of Keppelman a rumour that had started floating around the studio. It had started in the carpentry department and when Keppelman learned that the source was said to be one Lefty Klein, he was summoned to Keppelman's office.

There had been trouble with Klein in the past, in connection with his tendency to be up a ladder fixing the top of a partition in the region of the women's changing cubicles. On this occasion, however, Keppelman was prepared to overlook how he had come by his information.

So, when Klein started his alibi, 'I just happened to be up there fixing this fanlight. There'd been a lot of complaints about the draught whistling through there –' Keppelman broke in : 'Skip all that. I haven't got you in here to fire you. All I want is the facts, for the good of the future of the firm. We've got a lot of money invested in this, and if the rumour you've been putting around is true, this is castrastophic."

'It *is* true.'

'What is?'

'Helga Lemurr. She's as flat as a pancake.'

'What do you mean, flat as a pancake?'

'The busty substances. There's nothing there. Bee stings, that's all.'

'You're sure?'

'Positive.'

Keppelman fell into deep thought. And then a great dawning came upon him. This explained everything. Not allowing anyone near her but her personal dresser and maid. Turning thumbs down on the Malibu Beach stunt. Refusing to pose for any pin-ups.

'Okay, Klein, you can go.' Keppelman pressed the buzzer for his secretary. 'A meeting here. *Now*. Get 'em all in. This is top priority. Tell 'em to drop everything they're doing. Oh, my God, this is a disaster.'

The meeting had gone on for just on an hour with more and more gloom descending on the assembled company as the realisation that 'we'll go for broke on Helga Lemurr' now looked as though it was going to become all too shatteringly true. But then the woman in charge of the wardrobe department made the comment:

'We should get Titzling to see what he can do about it.'

'Titzling? Who's he?' asked Keppelman.

'Otto Titzling. You remember him. He's the man who made Dick Malone's body-belt for him.'

'Body-belt! What's body-belts got to do with it?'

'That's not Titzling's main thing. It was just a special job he did for Dick once when he was in New York. Titzling is normally women's underwear. He probably knows more about bras and bosoms than anyone else in the country. He's been in it longer than anyone else. He probably invented the bra.'

'He did,' said another woman present. 'If anyone can help us, it's Titzling. He's been working on boosters. The first ones he made weren't so hot. But I understand he's got a new line that –'

'Boosters?' said Keppelman. 'What the hell are boosters?'

'They're a sort of false bust. If somebody's flat-chested –'

'Get him,' said Keppelman, a man known for his quick decisions.

And so it was that Titzling was summoned to Hollywood. It was all shrouded in secrecy, with no hint of the real reason why Apex were calling him in, which they felt would have been fatal if it ever became known to the public. That was why from the moment Keppelman had heard the ghastly news he had made a jotting on his memo pad, 'Helga's bust must never come out', which caused his secretary to raise her eyebrows when she came upon it.

Staff loyalty at Apex was such that the damaging truth about Helga Lemurr's non-bosom never did become general knowledge. The falsies Titzling evolved for her, for wear under sweaters, in evening wear, and even for swimsuits, were so masterly that there was never a pin-up shot in which anyone could suspect that the Lemurr bust was anything but genuine.

It was a Hollywood secret as well kept as the fact that Rin Tin Tin, the wonder dog, was in truth a female, something which the producer could get away with in the majority of scenes – except for the final fade-out, with good old Rinty standing on a rock silhouetted against the sunset in all his (her) majesty. In such cases Rin Tin Tin had to wear a falsie.

"How long were you on the bra case?"

The lengthy Berlei-Bali lawsuit was a legal cause
célèbre. *Earlier, similar litigation had cost*
Titzling fame and fortune

11

Philippe de Brassière

Philippe de Brassière arrived in New York from Paris in the late
1920s to set himself up as a dress designer on Fifth Avenue. The news
columns of the newspapers signalled his arrival with stories of the
exploits of Capitaine de Brassière as an air ace in the Great War
and the women's pages joined with *Harper's Bazaar* and *Vogue* in
devoting much space to the launching of his collections. The tall,
suave Frenchman was lionised at the parties given specially for him
by New York society women. It was regarded as a great *coup* if you
could impress your friends by his accepting your invitation to come
to tea. He made a great hit and women had no hesitation in paying
the outlandish prices he charged for his creations.

But the Wall Street crash, as it did to many another whose business
was booming, knocked the debonair Capitaine for a loop. With so
many well-to-do husbands being wiped out financially or, worse

than that, being taken off to the morgue after the sound of a shot in the men's washroom, women who were pace-setters in the social world just did not have the money to spend on the gowns and dresses of Philippe de Brassière. But to his credit he was resourceful. He reasoned that since the Depression into which the nation had sunk was likely to continue for quite a period it would be a considerable time before anything as expensively unessential as *haute couture* could make a comeback. So, the smart thing to do would be to use what resources he had to switch right away to something, still in the field of women's wear if possible, which came under the heading of a necessity and which women had to buy, regardless.

Thus it was that he invaded Otto Titzling's territory and, as things turned out, 'invaded' was the apt word. Others who had set out to cash in on the lucrative field in which Titzling had pioneered put products of their own design on the market and, something for which Otto was thankful, invariably not as good as his. De Brassière, however, felt no need of seeking originality. Blatantly he copied the Titzling garments, merely flossing them up with the use of more fanciful materials and ornamentation and giving them intriguing French names.

Titzling had no option but to sue, even though it was not the best of times to get involved in the expense of litigation. He had only just weathered not only the Depression but also that earlier disaster to the trade – the Boyish or Flat-chested Look. Girls had been so obsessed in the mid-1920s with looking bustless that they had gone to the extent of battening themselves down with broad strips of adhesive of the type used for strapping broken ribs. Apart from the aesthetics of this, Otto was horrified at the thought of the agony it must have been when they ripped it off. He did switch some of his production to a flattening garment, but his heart wasn't in it. Sales went right down and didn't recover until the bust came back into its own at the beginning of the 1930s – just in time for the Depression. But he could not let Philippe de Brassière get away with the flagrant theft of his ideas and in due course he took him to court.

Titzling's attorney did not handle the case well, but this was in no small measure due to the fact that Otto had been remiss, away back in the days of Swanhilda, in not patenting the item he had evolved for her. He had been young then and not fully aware of the importance of immediately safeguarding, through the Patents Office, any new idea that had commercial possibilities. Later when the general demand had come for his brainchild and he had set up his company, he had hastened to patent all the modifications, new developments and variations in the wide range he put on the market. It made an impressive stack of photostats, affadavits, drawings and specifications for his lawyer to wave at their opponents in court. But de Brassière's attorney was quick to seize on to the point that the evidence looked terribly convincing but it had one big fault : where among all that raft of papers was the important, vital one – Titzling's patent for the garment itself? Titzling, it was argued, presented acceptable proof that his modifications were of his own copyright design but since he produced no similar proof that the article to which those modifications were made was also of his design one could only assume that it was in the common field, for anyone to copy without infringement of patents.

This move set Otto's lawyer back on his heels. He could only argue that it did not justify de Brassière in copying the many refinements in design which made it almost an entirely different article from the original concept, all such refinements being fully protected by patents. But he was arguing to an unsympathetic court. The Titzling action had been brought in regard to the garment itself, not just aspects of it. Why change course in midstream?

It was to no avail that the Titzling camp could draw to the attention of the court the fact that Philippe de Brassière was an imposter. He had not been, as claimed, a leading fashion designer in Paris along with Patou, Worth, Balenciaga and the others of that period. He had in fact come to New York to try his luck after having failed to make the grade in Paris. He had not turned to making women's underwear because the Depression had made things difficult for *haute couture*. The more simple reason was that his clothes had not stood the test in New York and his patrons, entranced at first, had drifted away when it was found that he was indeed a poor designer. And all that stuff about his being an air ace. Granted there was a photograph of him on leave in Cannes resplendent in his uniform, but who in America was to know that a chauffeur's uniform bore a close resemblance to that worn by French Air Force pilots? But all this well-documented shooting down of the Capitaine in flames was, on objection from his counsel, struck from the record as irrelevant.

The case was to revolve around the matter of patents and in the end Titzling did receive damages in regard to certain specific details of manufacture. But they were only token damages and he was not awarded costs. Philippe de Brassière had, in effect, won the case.

The litigation had been protracted, extending through involved legal argument, appeals and so forth to just on four years. In this time it attracted a great deal of publicity, due not a little to the fact that the Judge at the main hearings relished the subject matter of what was before him. It was a wonderful change from listening to contention about the manufacturing rights to a sausage machine, say, or the tedious facts and figures of a complicated fraud case. He expressed himself not satisfied merely to hear verbal discussion. He wanted the court to be able to see the pros and cons of the Titzling and de Brassière products demonstrated on live models. And as regards the space the papers naturally devoted to this, the Frenchman got much the better of the deal.

Titzling had Miss Wasserman model his items for him, and although she was sufficiently attractive and carried it off well enough when the Judge would ask them to approach the bench so that he could see more clearly the exact aspects of the garment under discussion, she just did not have the class or the flair of de Brassière's girl. He used Stephanie Belle-Chose, his top model whom he had brought with him from France when he had first come to New York. There was no question that she made her court appearance a performance, much to the annoyance of Otto and Hans and their legal advisers. The Titzling attorney was numerous times on his feet to object to the unfair, irrelevant tactics being used. The usual photographers on hand outside the court were greatly augmented in numbers when Stephanie was appearing and as they would carry her off for a special session of feature shots, Delving would comment bitterly : 'Off she goes in a cloud of lust.' He pleaded with Otto to let him get somebody who could similarly enliven their side of the case but Otto was against it degenerating into that sort of striving to outdo each other.

The result was that Stephanie, and therefore de Brassière's side of the case, got the big play in the public prints. The *Police Gazette*, of fond memory to many, was in there with a large blow-up of her in revealing pose, with the headline : 'I did it all for Bra.' She used the nickname by which he was known to all his intimates and it is interesting that this was the start of the general acceptance of the term 'bra', as well of course as the full word 'brassiere', as the way of referring to the article of women's underwear which by rights should still be called a 'titzling'. *The Dictionary of American Slang* lists 'bra' as having come into general usage in 1938 – the year in which the case ended.

Not only financially but in other respects this unsuccessful case could be said to have broken Titzling.

Elegant modelling contributed to Philippe de Brassière's success

Hettie Titzling, a maiden niece who was very helpful to the author in the gathering of his material for this book, said: 'Poor Uncle Otto. He was completely dispirited by the time it was all over. He felt all his life's work had gone for nothing. He lost interest. The firm went downhill and he just couldn't keep up the turnover required to bring in the money to pay off all his legal debts. Although it was awfully sad when he died when he wasn't all that old, at least he was spared seeing his company go into the hands of the receivers. It was such a pity. He was such a nice, kind man.'

With the Second World War then on, Hans Delving went into war work and was to rise to quite a prominent post in the Psychological Warfare Board, his knowledge of German being useful in what was one of their main functions – the preparation of propaganda leaflets for dropping over enemy territory. In the last year of the war he was one of those listed as missing when the plane in which he was flying to Europe was attacked over the Bay of Biscay.

Sheer Delight, *a Rose Lewis bra*

12

The Brassiere Today

From the simple beginnings of Otto Titzling's day the brassiere industry has grown to such an extent that in the U.S. now 170,000,000 are sold annually. In Britain every girl, mother and grandma, and also maiden ladies, buys on average two bras a year. By far the most popular colour is white, which outsells all other colours put together. Coming up fast, however, is what in mother's day was called 'flesh coloured' or 'tea rose', but which is now dubbed 'skin tone'. What helps to give 'skin tone' an authentic ring is, of course, the fact that the material is so sheer that the skin itself shows through. Extremely flimsy as it is – held in the hand, only a slight breeze is enough to waft it away – what puzzles the male public is how manufacturers can charge as much and more than the price of a pair of trousers for something so inconsequential. The manufacturers' reply to this is that the more fine the fabric the more careful must be the craftsmanship that goes into it. And, after all, there are always at least nineteen component parts that have to be stitched together, no matter how much of a 'nothing bra' it may look.

Although black, third on the best-seller list, is a great favourite with men, especially when buying a present for an intimate friend, women themselves are comparatively rare purchasers of this colour, for a reason which men don't think of. It has very restricted use. It cannot be worn with a white or any light-coloured blouse or sweater, because of the unattractive show-through. As one leading corsetiere put it : 'Black underwear is great for undressing in front of your boy friend, but for little else.'

Religion has a close bearing on bra colours. In Ireland and other strictly Catholic countries the big seller is still the bright pink rayon satin bra of grandma's time. Anything more racy is almost but not quite likely to be confiscated by Customs officials along with the works of Henry Miller. Corsetieres also find they have difficulty in displaying their wares properly in regions where Catholicism is strong. In Canada manufacturers for years had to have separate advertising posters for Quebec Province. Models had to dangle a length of tulle in front of their bust, so that potential women purchasers could get an inkling of what the bra looked like without any danger of male excitation.

On file in the offices of the Silhouette company is a letter from an Irish woman which bears testimony to the religious aspect of underwear :

'I don't know what possessed me to do it but on Tuesday I bought some of your black underwear, the Magic Moments Pantee Corselet, to be precise. I have never worn black under garments before in my life and you can believe me when I say that I will never do so again. The day I wore it for the first time, which was the day before yesterday, when I got undressed in the evening I found that I had come out in a rash. And I knew at once that I was being punished for my sinfulness. I prayed to the Good Lord for forgiveness and have been to confession and the Priest said that he hoped that God in his infinite mercy would forgive this transgression, provided I was truly penitent and would never again harbour such thoughts that would prompt me to do such a thing again. I hope so much that this will prove true, although as yet the rash does not look to be clearing up.

Sincerely yours,

(Mrs) ——— ———

P.S.   I enclose the corselet of which I write and in view of the fact that as indicated above it has been barely worn I am sure you will see your way clear to refund me the purchase price.'

The bra manufacturers invite mothers to believe that they should get their daughters into bras by the time they are ten or so. This is nothing more nor less than a con game, designed to boost sales. In advertisements they trot out all sorts of seemingly convincing arguments that have mothers thinking that if they don't slap a bra on to little Elsie the moment things start to get moving on her upper chest they will be condemning the poor youngster to a droopy future. And as far as the little girls are concerned the manufacturers give their junior brassieres such names as the Grow-Bra, instilling into the innocent child the idea that once donned the garment will, as if by magic, start them growing and growing until in no time she will have breasts just like mummy's, or with luck better.

Doctors, except those getting a retainer as 'Medical Consultant' to a bra company, don't go along with this thesis. Dr Derek Llewellyn-Jones, in his book *Everywoman*, is just one of the many who dismiss the whole thing as ridiculous, for the simple reason that 'there is no danger of drooping and little to which to give uplift'.

As we all know, the basic sizes of brassieres, ranging from 32 to 40 inches, are the four cup sizes A, B, C and D, or as they are known in the trade, eggcup, teacup, coffee cup and Challenge Cup. But what is not generally known is that whereas 'average' in the bra business for many a year has meant a 34-inch bust, today it is going closer and closer to 36. 'Breasts are getting bigger,' any manufacturer will tell you, albeit with mixed feelings since on the one hand he is the bearer of good tidings and on the other it will be necessary for him to say to his works manager. 'We're going to have to bump up our production on the 36s', which will mean lowering of profit margin through use of extra material. And his explanation for the increase in size will be simple : 'It's the Pill.'

But this is not borne out by medical science, for the obvious reason that it would be a strange paradox if a pill designed for the avoidance of pregnancy should induce the breast-swelling associated with that condition. In truth the explanation is that we are better physical specimens that our predecessors were, through better nutrition, higher standard of living bringing better diet for all, improved working conditions, holidays in the sun and fresh air for everybody, etc. Statistics associated with rugby football players, for example, show that members of modern rugger teams are on average an inch and a half taller and two stones heavier than those of the 1920s. If better nutrition and so on can do that for football players, it's a certainty that also it must do something for the bust.

In fashion modelling, the girls who go beyond just displaying clothes and have to strip down to model bras get extra money. They call it their booby prize.

Some modern trends. Delving would doubtless have approved

It is a general misconception among women that too much washing makes the rubber in foundation garments deteriorate. Quite the opposite is the case. The more they are washed the longer life they are assured. It is not the washing that plays havoc with the rubber. It is the effect of the body acids on it. Washing clears them of such acids and keeps to a minimum the harmful effects they have. So one shouldn't pay too much attention to the star of the television commercial who pulls and pushes and prods a bra and says how wonderful it is that it is still in great shape after no fewer than 65 washings. Certainly a bra will stand up well to 65 washings, a bra expert will tell you knowingly, but get someone to wear it in between the washings – ah, that's the real test.

The brassiere people make special tests to arrive at the precise effect perspiration has on the rubber content, as well as the staining action on coloured fabrics. Research chemists, after a long process of trial and error, have managed to isolate the chemical components of B.O. It can now be reproduced synthetically by mixing in solution 0.5 grammes of histidine mono-hydrochloride mono-hydrate with 2.5 g of disodium hydrogen orthophosphate per litre and bringing it up to pH 8.0 with 0.1 N sodium hydroxide. That of course is alkaline B.O. If you want the acid variety you change the formula by using 2.2 grammes of disodium hydrogen orthophosphate. Having mixed one or the other of these solutions in what they call the 'perspirometer', the garment to be tested is then immersed in it. After a good soaking it is then placed in an oven at 37 $\pm$ 2°C. (100 $\pm$ 4°F.), which is the equivalent of blood heat, for four hours or more.

When the author visited the Silhouette factory he was fortunate, or unfortunate depending on how you look at it, in arriving in the testing lab as they were taking a fresh batch out of the oven. Overpowering. I found it difficult to concentrate on what the girl in charge of the operation was telling me about varying the time spent in the oven so as to make it the equivalent of a hard-fought game of tennis or an all-night session in an ill-ventilated discotheque. My head was swimming. Even the staff don't get completely acclimatised. After a time it is found necessary to switch them to another department for a breather.

It is a hard life for the girls in the Testing and Quality Control Department, since apart from having to pore over underwear exuding synthetic B.O. there are the perpetual day-in-day-out sound effects. The churn-churn-churn of the washing machines putting the various garments to washing tests is not too bad, it being a sound to which one gets conditioned by visits to the neighbourhood launderette. But the Kelston Resilience Testing Machine is a different matter altogether. This bulky machine has two metal arms to which is attached a piece a stretch fabric or elastic. The controls are set to give the desired length of stretch, the machine turned on, and the two arms pull the material out and let it whip back to normal over and over again.

Indeed a handy gadget to simulate the wear and tear on, say, the elastic side panel of a bra during the day-to-day activities of the wearer. But one wonders why it has to be so noisy about it. The loud metallic click-clack-click-clack reverberates throughout the department.

'How many stretches do you give it?' I asked the young lady at the helm. 'A thousand or so?'

'Good heavens, no,' she said. 'Far more than that.'

I looked at the counter on the side and it was showing over 84,000 for the particular piece of bra being tested.

'You see,' she went on, 'we're trying to find out the point of breakdown and it goes on until that is reached.'

'It would drive me crazy,' I remarked to one of the girls making a sea-water test on a bikini-top. 'Me too,' she said, with the heartfelt feeling of one longing for the *twang* that would signal the arrival of breakdown point.

One of the biggest bra companies is Berlei and it was founded by an Australian named Burley, who was to be joined by the man who was to become chairman, named Hurley. There are few unable to resist the temptation of referring to the Hurley-Burley of the bra business when one sees some 250 girls at a Berlei factory in one vast room rat-tat-tatting away at their machines as the conveyor belts whisk their bits and pieces back and forth to the finishers. So specialised is the work that a girl can, for example, do nothing else all day but machine the five stitches needed to join a shoulder strap to a bra cup. One would think the monotony of it would drive them out of their minds, but oddly enough it has been found that if a girl is put on to another operation by way of a change, sooner or later

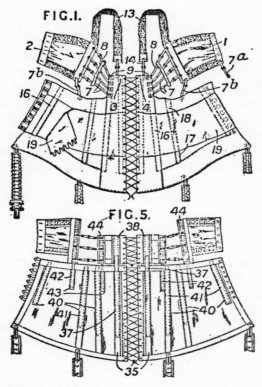

Machining underwear can be a complex business, as this diagram of over 40 component pieces shows

it's 'I want to get back to underarm gussets' or whatever she had been on before.

It is strange that a firm as efficient as Berlei would have a lapse whereby they call one of their brassieres *Ophelia*. Were he alive now, Fred Burley, whose memory is so revered that they are always quoting his aphorisms with the preamble 'Dead Fred said –', would certainly never have let that one slip through. Granted in the trade there is a liking for what Hans Delving called catchy selling sentences, as with Silhouette's 'Why be bouncy running for a bus?' and fashion designer Mary Quant does call her padded bras *Quantities*, but *Ophelia* is rather near the knuckle.

The Queen's brassieres are made by Rigby and Peller Ltd of Mayfair and they proudly display their 'By Appointment' crest at their place of business and in their advertisements. Naturally they would not dream of discussing for publication any details of what might be termed the Royal Enclosure. But from other sources one learns that, for the best of reasons, they had the devil's own time when preparing their contribution to the Queen's appearance for her Coronation. Her Majesty is of a build which, in normal circumstances, a corsetiere would enhance to its full advantage. Reluctantly, however, they had to opt for understatement, since after all the focal point of interest had to be the placing of the crown on her head.

A well-known character in the business is Rose Lewis. She says of her lingerie shop : 'It is a landmark of Knightsbridge. There isn't a taxi driver in London who doesn't know it.' One can well understand this. Her main creation is a bare-look brassiere and although these are merely displayed on dummies in the window, there are few taxi drivers who could pass by without having a vivid impression imprinted on their minds of the impact when worn.

Rose, a Middle-European lady who has been in the brassiere business for more than twenty years, calls her specialty the Open Plan Bra. To the casual observer it appears to be nothing more nor less than two triangles of tape, with shoulder straps and with a band around the bottom to attach at the back. A breast is inserted into each open triangle and the effect when the contraption is pulled tight and fastened securely has to be seen to be believed. For more than one person who has been in a position to observe the effect the Guns of Navarone have immediately come to mind.

However, one should not run away with the idea that Rose Lewis designed her bra with the intention of its being sexy. In her thick Hungarian accent she will tell you that the whole idea of the thing is for the welfare of the wearer. She designed it that way for health reasons. 'It is extremely bad,' she says, 'to have the flesh of the bosoms constantly encased, especially in the padded fabrics of today. The skin cannot breathe normally as it should, and eventually the breasts will shrivel up.'

Which just shows how misunderstandings can arise. The majority of her clients do not realise that they are buying a health garment. It is doubtful whether the titled gentlemen and well-to-do business-men are aware of it when they finance young ladies of their acquaintance for a Rose Lewis bra, at a starting price of £6.30 for the standard job. Women of the entertainment world – both enter-tainment worlds – might but probably don't have a fear of their breasts shrivelling up. And there is certainly only one reason why she gets so many society women coming into her shop saying : 'My husband keeps at me that I really must do something about myself.'

An interesting thing about this is that it reflects how what are regarded as respectable women have in today's permissive society overcome innate dislike of drawing attention to two portions of their anatomy. One was that gap above the stocking-tops. Psychiatrists will tell you that the sense of decency that prompted them at all costs to avoid anybody ever seeing it was the prime reason for men getting so excited about it, just as seeing an ankle in Victorian times was really something. The advent of what the British call tights and Americans call pantie-hose has changed all that, even though it is not so much that women have overcome their concern about stocking-tops as that they virtually don't exist any more.

The other focal point of their self-consciousness has always been the nipples. Low-cut dresses and clinging sweaters they would wear without a shred of embarrassment, revel in them, in fact. But in the past (except for the distant past as in the time of the Renaissance or the ancient Greeks and Romans) they would draw the line at the nipples, even if merely observed in outline on dress or sweater. But today we are in the permissive era of frontal display, not only on stage and screen, but also even in our family newspapers, especially the Sundays, where the nipple count is high. This cannot help but have an influence on ordinary women, as against those who are in the entertainment world or photographic modelling and who are, as it were, in the business of display.

More and more the office girl, housewife, society gal is getting around to the feeling that the nipple-taboo has gone by the board. And the big commercial bra-makers, as well as specialists like Rose Lewis and the 'Dare you wear this?' advertisers in the soft-porn mags, are catering to this. One reputable firm presents theirs as 'the bra that gives you push-up without cover-up'. Although this is no novelty to showbiz types such as Jayne (Thanks for the Mammary) Mansfield and new bombshell Julie Ege, it is such a new departure for the ordinary woman who now wants to get into the swing of things that when she goes into a store to buy one she doesn't quite know what to ask for. Usually they fall back on asking for it by cup size. On the basis of the Half Cup being a cleavage-revealing bra, they call this newcomer to general wear the Quarter Cup.

One feels sure that if our friends Otto Titzling and Hans Delving were alive today they would have put their heads together to think of a good name for this one, with Hans doubtless getting a sudden inspiration : 'Why wouldn't a girl say to herself, "I'll call it my Happiness Bra, because my cup runneth over." ?'